First edition, 2011

Published by The Southern Illinoisan
Printed by Walsworth Publishing Co., Marceline, Mo.

Hardcover edition ISBN 13: 978-0-615-52945-5

Why Worry When You Can Pray?

The Life and Faith of Rosemary Crisp

By Tom Woolf
Foreword by Brenda Edgar

Rosemary Berkel Crisp.

Foreword

Rosemary Crisp was a remarkable woman. She will be remembered for her philanthropic endeavors and volunteer work, her effervescent personality and the deep, abiding faith that kept her strong for those around her as she fought cancer.

In the last years of her life, Rosemary was an inspiration to me and to everyone who knew her. She taught us that every day is a gift to be lived as well and happily as possible.

One of the last times I visited with Rosemary was the day after Thanksgiving 2006. I had heard that her time was getting short, and I wanted to spend time with her before she became too weak for guests. When Jim and I arrived at Crisp Acres, the red Colonial mansion in Marion, we were welcomed and invited into the den. When Harry L. walked in, he explained that Rosemary was at the hospital receiving a treatment and would be home soon.

After we had a "catch-up" visit and a Diet Pepsi with Harry L., Rosemary returned home. She looked beautiful, just as she always did. She was wearing a red leather jacket and dangling from her wrist was a bracelet with charms, each one of the silhouette heads representing a grandchild and her great-grandchild. She proudly explained that it was a Mother's Day gift. She adored her family.

After our chat in the den, she asked if we would like to see the new stable; the old one had been destroyed in a fire. As we walked along the road from the house to the stable, Rosemary told me that she knew she was living on borrowed time, but she was going to make the most of that time.

We walked into the immaculate stall areas and patted the horses. We walked into the great room, which was designed by Rosemary for entertaining family and friends. There was a pool table and a ping pong table, and an enormous fireplace for warmth, with a large television hung over it for viewing. There were places for quiet conversation and a large dining table where the entire family had enjoyed Thanksgiving dinner the day before. She had seen to every detail.

The spacious kitchen had the perfect spot for one of Rosemary's pencil drawings of a mother horse and her baby in a tranquil pasture. There also were a few leftovers, and we were offered some of the Crisp family's traditional holiday cranberry frappé. It was delicious, and I asked Rosemary for the recipe. It arrived in the mail with a note sometime later.

After the note arrived, I was sitting alone in our home, reflecting on our last visit. I thought I shouldn't have asked her for that recipe. She surely didn't need to be copying recipes and mailing them. I knew how advanced her cancer was, and I was awed by her grace, courage, perseverance, thoughtfulness and ever-present positive attitude. How did she do it? As I was praying for her, I was moved to call her and suggest she write a book. Perhaps, I thought, we could learn from Rosemary.

I found the phone number for their home in the Florida Keys. I was a bit reluctant to call, fearing she might not feel well enough to talk. But when she came to the phone, I asked if we could talk for just a couple of minutes.

"Why yes," she answered. "I have a few minutes. Then I'm off to a committee meeting." Committee meeting? And I was worried she might not be strong enough for a short phone conversation! I explained how I had been stirred to call her and let her know I thought she should write a book. (Why would I dare ask her to write a book when I wondered how she felt like copying a recipe and mailing it?) She said others had suggested that, as well. We talked a few more minutes, and she was off to her meeting.

The next time I saw Rosemary was in August 2007, nine months after what I had expected to be our last visit. There she was, out and about and looking lovely. She sat next to me in the grandstand at the Du Quoin State Fairgrounds during the World Trotting Derby harness race. She told me about the cruise they had taken and that she was working on her book. I told her I was glad she was writing. But a cruise? How did she do it? Again, I was filled with awe. She was nearing the end of a fabulous life, but she hadn't stopped living.

In November, I received a phone message from Rosemary, which is still on my machine. She asked me to write the foreword for her book. I was humbled and honored.

Rosemary was a remarkable woman. She knew she was living on borrowed time, but she kept on going for Harry L. and Cathy, Cyndi, Cheryl, Carole, Cara and Lee, and for her grandchildren, the rest of her family and her many, many friends. Although we may not acknowledge it, we are all living on borrowed time. Rosemary showed us how to live each day we are given.

Brenda Edgar
Former First Lady of Illinois (1991-1999)
Charleston, Illinois

The Crisps in Clark, Colo., on a family trip: Cathy, Carole, Rosemary, Harry 'Lee,' Harry L., Cheryl, Cara and Cyndi.

Introduction

Children everywhere grow up hearing from their parents, "Do as I say, not as I do."

It wasn't quite that way for Cynthia, Catherine, Cheryl, Carole, Lee and Cara, the children of Rosemary and Harry L. Crisp II.

Because their mom always seemed to be saying and doing the right things.

For them.

For her husband.

And for everyone else around her.

She really was that good. Rosemary Crisp was blessed with many talents, talents she gladly shared in a very honest – and humble – way to make the world a better place, to raise the spirits of those she encountered, to help others achieve their goals. Her positive outlook, her energy and her passion were infectious.

For generations, home base for the Crisp family has been Marion, Ill., a busy community bisected by Interstate 57, two hours southeast of St. Louis. Rosemary's spirituality, compassion and generosity of deed and spirit are well known in Marion and throughout the part of the state known as Southern Illinois. And beyond.

She really never was interested in the spotlight. Trite as it may seem, she genuinely cared about others. No effort was too big, no gesture too insignificant. Father Richard Mohr vividly recalls the first Mass he celebrated in July 1990 as the new priest at St. Joseph's Catholic Church in Marion, Rosemary's church since childhood. There she was to greet him with a warm smile and a welcoming handshake. A day later, a supply of Pepsi products showed up at his doorstep; his parishioner, who also happened to be the co-owner of Pepsi MidAmerica in Marion, wanted to make sure her new priest and his housekeeper had enough soda.

When Southeast Missouri State University in Cape Girardeau needed guidance and leadership in its effort to secure accreditation for its nursing school, officials there turned to Rosemary. With her training in and love of nursing, her affection for the university and her commitment to helping others achieve their life dreams, she was only too happy to help. The building that houses Southeast's School of Nursing bears her name. While

A young Rosemary, with brother Jim, strikes a pretty pose.

anyone familiar with her tireless efforts would agree it was a well-deserved honor, it was never Rosemary's goal.

The person who knew her best, Harry L., says his wife of nearly 48 years loved people, loved life, and she cared about her community and country. "It was never about her. It was always about others."

Violette 'Mimi' Crisp, Harry L.'s mother, and Rosemary hold hands at a stop during a tour of London.

She touched the lives of thousands through her service to numerous organizations at the national, state and local levels, many related to education and to health. One of her greatest sources of pride was the annual Southern Illinois Women's Health Conference, which she co-founded in 1986 and which continues to grow in popularity.

Rosemary had a positive impact on people, even though they never knew it. One of her trademark habits was to "tidy up" in public restrooms. It didn't matter where she was. She would wipe down sinks and pick up paper towels left lying on the floor. Everyone who knows the story admits – always with a chuckle – that either they do the same thing, or, at the minimum, think of Rosemary when they enter a public restroom.

Outside of family and close friends, no one knew she did that. Brenda Edgar, former First Lady of Illinois, believes it reflected the essence of her dear friend.

"That was her way of finding a way to stay in touch with who she was. She made a decision she was going to leave the restroom cleaner than when she found it. And that is how she lived her life – to leave it nice for the next person and do it anonymously. It made her happy."

Her belief system sprang, of course, from the foundation her parents provided. The youngest of four children, Rosemary grew up in Southern Illinois in a home of modest means. Albert and Rose Berkel's home was filled with love, and they instilled in Delores, Pat, Jim and Rosemary the importance of faith, family and hard work.

From this solid start in life, Rosemary created and maintained the same foundation for her own family. Together with Harry L., her best friend and confidant, they filled their lives with the joys – and yes, certainly the demands – of a growing family and a growing business. Whatever the challenges, Rosemary and Harry L. relied on each other.

"As our lives evolved, to this very day we are true partners," Rosemary said. "He is my best friend. I'd marry him again in a minute. He says when I hurt, he hurts. We've cried together, we've laughed together. We truly just like being together."

They faced an unexpected challenge in 1975 when the then 38-year-old mother learned she had cervical cancer. Ever selfless, Rosemary's thoughts immediately turned to her family.

"I wanted to cry. I felt like the door to my life had just been closed. We had six children, ages 15 to younger than 2. They needed me."

Harry L. was at her side at Mayo Clinic in Rochester, Minn. Upon hearing the word cancer, he remembers thinking it instantly meant death.

"We had recently had our sixth child; we had our hands full in every way, with our business and at home. For me, panic probably set in, concern for her, concern for the kids. She was brave from the start, and being such a devout Catholic, she said, 'Why worry when you can pray?' She followed that philosophy, and her enormous strength gave me strength. She was, very quietly, a very strong woman."

Like her husband, Rosemary thought she had been given a death sentence. As was her custom, she turned to Harry L.

"My husband said, 'We'll work it out together.' He helped me get through it."

Surgery was successful, and Rosemary soon resumed what for her was a normal pace, devoting her time and efforts to her passions – her family, the business, her circle of friends, community service and, of course, her church. As her mother used to say, Rosemary always had her "get-up-and-go pants on." With all that she wanted

Rosemary helps prepare Thanksgiving dinner with daughters Cara and Cyndi (left) and daughter-in-law Stacie, at Cyndi's home in Paducah, Ky.

Rosemary and Harry L. are surrounded by their grandchildren.

to accomplish each day, she surely needed those pants. But they were a natural fit.

She quite simply was always doing for others. Sometimes it involved nursing; she was a volunteer Red Cross nurse for the blood mobile for 15 years, and for five years was a volunteer Girl Scout camp nurse. When eldest daughter Cyndi came home heartbroken one day, tearfully telling her mom that there was no leader for her Brownie troop, Rosemary stepped in. She may not have anticipated her tenure as a troop leader spanning 12 years, but she embraced the role because she loved children and loved serving as a mentor. As her children grew, so did her volunteer efforts, particularly in the areas of health and education.

Pepsi MidAmerica also was growing. A business that started on the back of a truck that Harry L.'s dad had used to haul chickens and eggs, eventually expanded to supply products to three states, then to five. Success created through hard work and sacrifice also translated into well-deserved opportunities for Rosemary and Harry L. Their travels took them around the country and around the world, meeting presidents and popes along the way. Condos they purchased in Key Largo, Fla., were a get-away not only for immediate and extended family, but also for friends; the Crisps' door was always open.

Life, of course, is unpredictable; its ebb and flow can create joy and sorrow, triumph and disappointment, satisfaction and chagrin. At times, most everyone faces unexpected challenges, and Rosemary was no different. She met them straight on, relying on her deep faith, her abundant common sense and wisdom to help her find solutions.

But in December 1995, Rosemary began another new – and unexpected – journey. On a visit to Cooper Clinic in Dallas, Texas, a physician noticed during a routine examination that her right ovary was enlarged. Their trusted doctor, Larry Gibbons, suggested it might be a benign ovarian cyst and recommended further testing. He agreed with Rosemary's idea of follow-up testing at Mayo Clinic. Ever optimistic and equipped with the knowledge that came with her years as a registered nurse, Rosemary wasn't overly concerned.

Harry L., Rosemary's husband of nearly 48 years, says his wife loved people. 'It was never about her,' he says. 'It was always about others.'

"I am the eternal optimist," she said later, recalling the initial diagnosis. "I don't worry about something until they tell me that I have something to worry about. I feel worry is just using a lot of energy, and when you do need that energy you're too zapped to think logically about it. So, no, I really didn't worry so much."

The follow-up tests took place in Rochester, Minn., on Dec. 14. While there was no question the cyst would have to be removed, her doctors said the procedure could wait until after the holidays. Surgery was on Jan. 31, 1996.

"I had made my family promise me that in the event that this was malignant, I wanted to be told up front. I wanted to know about it. I didn't want to hear it from out in the hallway or something like that. I remember being in my room, and when I came to, the kids were lining the bed. And they said, 'Mother, you're back in your room and things went well.' I looked at my daughter Cyndi, knowing I wanted the truth, and she said, 'Well, Mother, it was malignant, but things are going to be fine.'"

So began an odyssey that served as an inspiration to all who knew what she had to endure. Her doctors told her she had one to five years to live. But Rosemary wasn't defeated. Despite the difficult path she would have to travel, she was determined. In addition to the regular chemo and radiation treatments and all of their side effects, Rosemary developed other complications that required additional procedures and treatments, a number of them on a daily basis. Yet those who weren't aware of her illness never would have known. Rosemary carried herself with grace and dignity, and the pace she maintained was admirable. There were bad days, hard days, exhausting days, but she wouldn't slow down. In fact, she was just as active, if not more so, than she had been. Many times she would receive treatment at Mayo Clinic during the day, only to be on time for a meeting or an event in Southern Illinois the same evening. Rosemary enjoyed shopping, especially for others, and to this day, family members and friends continue to marvel at her stamina. Whether it was in Southern Illinois, in New York or overseas, while those around her wanted to stop and rest, Rosemary pressed on. On one occasion, Rosemary had chemo in the morning, then went for pizza and to the mall for some Christmas shopping. She always found unique gifts for all of her children and friends. It helped keep her mind focused on others rather than on herself. Her spirit was indomitable, her courage remarkable.

Rosemary had her private moments of anguish. But she refused to give in. Molly Norwood, a close friend and a breast cancer survivor, was among many who drew strength from Rosemary.

"She told me that she allowed herself 15 minutes a day for her own pity party. I remember asking her if I could save them up so that I could stay in bed a whole day and be mad at the world. She told me, 'Of course not. Sometimes I even set a timer to be sure I don't go beyond 15 minutes.'"

As she always had done, Rosemary relied on her family and her friends and, most importantly, her deep faith.

"I just say to God, 'I put it in your hands. Just use me. When I'm hurting, I think of Jesus, what you went through with your crucifixion, I just offer this up to you.' I don't ask why. He gives me such peace."

By the fall of 2007, Rosemary's condition was declining. Rosemary, Harry L. and daughter Cathy traveled to Mayo Clinic to meet with Rosemary's physician and close friend, Dr. Brigitte Barrette, to learn the results of the latest round of tests.

In a handwritten note that described the results, Rosemary wrote, "Today, Oct. 30th, 2007, is the day I will always remember." She had just learned that nothing more could be done.

Toward the end of November, Rosemary was hospitalized. Family and friends kept vigil, sharing memories and praying together. Weak though she may have been, her focus, as always, was not on herself. Friends from her past and her current friends came and went. Employees of Pepsi MidAmerica were asked to come to her room to receive instructions about replacing shrubbery in front of the Crisp Acres home, and she even met with someone who wanted an interview. To this day, son Lee shakes his head in disbelief. "Most people would be, 'Woe is me,'" he says, smiling warmly.

While everyone around Rosemary worried about her, she regretted how her passing might affect the family's holidays.

"She was afraid that would interfere then and in the future with everybody's Christmas," her husband says. "She wasn't thinking about dying because she knew she would be with God. She was worried about me, she was worried about how this would affect our Christmas. All of her thoughts were about others."

Rosemary passed on Dec. 1, 2007, at the age of 70. Father Mohr shed tears as he celebrated the funeral Mass on Dec. 6, calling his faithful parishioner and close friend an "apostle to the apostles." There were no limits to how she would reach out to others, he told those assembled, using the words of poet Edna St. Vincent Millay to express the feelings of everyone in St. Joseph's Catholic Church that day: "The presence of her absence is everywhere."

Yet, her spirit is everlasting. Two Christmas seasons later, Harry L. received a holiday card from a Goreville, Ill., woman who was a member of a Girl Scout troop that Rosemary led.

"This girl was a young teenager at the time and Rosemary took her under her wing," he says. "As a girl, this woman spent a lot of time with our daughters at our house before her family moved away. I get a Christmas card from her now; a woman in Rosemary's Girl Scouts 40 years ago. You can influence and touch people, as Rosemary did, and be a positive influence on many, many people. Or you can be a bad influence and never even know it. But Rosemary was a good influence on all of us. She made all of us better than we would have been."

Her life was, indeed, an inspiring journey.

Florida was one of Rosemary's favorite places to visit. This was taken at Lauderdale by the Sea.

With grandchildren (clockwise from top left) Olivia Rabbitt, Hunter Dickens, Ryan Rabbitt, Harrison Dickens, Alexandra Rabbitt, Hayden Dickens and Taylor Rabbit.

Harry L. and Rosemary in 1961.

Rosemary always greeted her family and friends at the door. She also made it a point to bid them farewell the same way.

Rosemary's 70th birthday — her last — was celebrated at a 'Hats Off to You, Rosemary' party in Florida in February 2007. Because of her health, the family considered cancelling the party, but she refused to miss it, greeting each guest one by one as they came through the door. A chair was provided for her, just in case she became tired, but she hardly took a minute to rest in it.

Rosemary and her brother, Jim Berkel, blow out the candles on their shared birthday cake. The two always celebrated together, because they were born one year and a day apart. She was 70.

Table of Contents

Early Years

Rosemary, the fourth child of Albert and Rosalee Berkel, takes a washpan bath.

'In every conceivable manner, the family
is the link to our past, and the bridge to our future.'
– Writer Alex Haley

When Rosemary took a personality test, the results revealed a woman with both drive and patience.

A patient Type A personality? At first glance, that might seem to be a contradiction in terms. But she was her parents' daughter.

"My mother was a role model," Rosemary said. "She was organized, very, very loving. She loved life, loved to garden, she worked for the hospital, she belonged to the women's club; she was a doer. My father was a loving man very humble to the point of being pretty meek. He only had a third-grade education. I learned to really appreciate him more in my adult years when I considered the sacrifices he made for all of us kids."

Organized. Loving. Loved life. A doer. Sacrifices. Sounds a great deal like the woman Rose and Albert Berkel's fourth child would grow up to be.

Rosalee Catherine Bayles and Albert James Berkel had three children – Delores Jean, age 7, Joanna Patricia (Pat), 2½, and Albert James Jr. (Jim), 1 – when Rosemary Ann joined the family. It was a brisk Feb. 22, 1937, in Chicago, and home at that time was an upstairs flat, heated with coal. Adjacent to train tracks, the children enjoyed collecting coal from the track bed.

Although the family lived in Chicago when Rosemary was born, Rose and Albert's roots were in Southern Illinois.

Albert was born in Equality. Around the age of 9, his mother died tragically in childbirth. Albert was sent from one family to another, living with whoever at the time could take care of him, so he was able to obtain only a third-grade

Rosemary and her brother, Jim, at the Military Ball at Rolla, Mo., in 1956.

education. Rose grew up not far away, in Creal Springs, Ill., where she graduated high school. After they married, they moved to Chicago, hoping to find more job opportunities; they, like people everywhere, were struggling under the weight of the Great Depression. Albert had experience as a carpenter, as his dad was a home builder and a farmer. That experience served him well, and Albert was able to get a job with the Chicago, Aurora & Elgin train line, working as a finish carpenter in their Chicago offices and remodeling the company's stations.

The family lived in Chicago until Rosemary was about 2, when they relocated to Creal Springs.

"My parents were both from that area, and I think they wanted to get out of the city and raise their family, instead of in a city atmosphere," Rosemary said.

Times, of course, were difficult, and the family would remain in Creal Springs for only two or three years. The economy continued to cause great pain for many families, and then the world was at war. Jim recalls their father working in an underground coal mine and learning welding skills, but Albert's desire to do better for his family prompted him to go to Evansville, Ind., to take a Navy welding test. Welders were needed for the ships being built at the shipyards on the Ohio River. So, after passing the

The Berkels and spouses: (Seated) Rosemary Berkel Crisp, Jim and Sue Berkel; (standing) Harry L. Crisp II, Delores Berkel McCuan, Mac McCuan, Pat Berkel Pulley, Barney Pulley, Rosemary's cousin Gloria Glaser and Barney Glaser.

test, the Berkel family moved to Evansville, about 85 miles northeast.

"Things were tough then, and we kids didn't want to leave our friends," Jim says. "But Dad needed a job, and this was a good-paying job for him, and he would be out of the danger of the coal mines."

Albert was a welder on LSTs – Landing Ship Tanks designed to carry and deploy supplies, vehicles and troops – that saw heavy use in the Pacific and in Europe. Albert's shipyard launched two LSTs every week; they were part of the largest amphibious force in the history of warfare that assaulted Omaha Beach on D-Day, June 6, 1944.

Jim remembers that his dad kept a memento of the Navy welding test. In one section of that test, Albert had to weld two 1½-inch pieces of steel end to end. To test its strength, the welded piece would be bent 170 degrees. If it didn't crack, you got the job. He got the job and kept the welded piece to remember.

After a few years, the family moved back to Marion. Because of the difficulty of finding a home, they initially settled in a housing project. Later, Albert and Rose bought a home on North State Street, where Rosemary spent most of her years growing up.

Resourcefulness was among the many traits the Berkel children learned. "We always had a garden, so Mom would can a lot of food and store it in a pantry," Jim recalls. "Mason jars and sealed lids were a must around our home. Mom could stretch a dollar, and we always had food for the table."

Childhood was a very happy time because of what Jim describes as "true family relationships."

"We ate together, we went to church together, we did everything together."

Albert Berkel and his children (clockwise from top) Delores, Rosemary, Jim and Pat.

Jim's closest relationship was with his little sister, perhaps because they were only a year apart.

"We had similar thoughts. Many times I knew what she was doing and thinking, and the same with her. We worked together a lot. I was the only boy, so I got different kinds of

A young Rosemary poses with a 'friend.'

This Berkel family portrait was taken for the 50th anniversary of Albert and Rose (center). Their children are Rosemary (left), Delores (right), Pat and Jim (standing). The painting on the wall was painted by Rosemary and was on display in her parents' home for many years.

Rosemary competes in the evening gown portion of the Miss Marion beauty pageant in 1959.

Rosemary (left) and her cousin, Patsy Berkel.

The Berkel siblings Jim and Rosemary (front) and Pat and Delores.

chores, but we all helped each other. If I needed any help, I could go to her. Whether it was while we were growing up or later on in life, we got things done together. She played off my mechanical skills, and I played off of her good nature.

"She taught me a lot of things, mostly respect. You know the old saying about the Golden Rule? She lived that. She didn't hold a grudge, she took what was dealt to her. She had a true honesty about her." And Rosemary dearly loved her big brother.

They had wonderful memories of the aromas and tastes of childhood – homemade ice cream, cinnamon rolls, cakes and pies; chicken and dumplings, and roast. As the youngest of three girls, Rosemary wore hand-me-downs for the most part, but that wardrobe, in fact, was a badge of honor.

"I looked at it that I was getting bigger, and I was getting to grow into my big sisters' sizes, so I can't remember feeling negative about that at all. I remember my Mother sewing some. We had a cow, and we had chickens, and, of course, we would buy feed. In those days, they had very colorful feed bags and with me being smaller, Mother would make pinafores out of the feed bags after they were washed. And really, they were quite cute. For special occasions, I did get a new dress, and, of course, we got new shoes."

Life revolved around family and church. The family drove to the Catholic church in nearby Stonefort every Sunday for Mass. The rest of the day was spent with relatives; the Berkels, Aunt Nell and Uncle John Agers, and their children, Joe, James, Johnny, Gloria and Tom, often gathered to share the large noon meal and conversation.

"We never had a discipline problem in our family," Rosemary recalled. "We were expected to have good manners, and we sat at the table until everybody was finished. Then they cleared the table. Sometimes, we would

Rosemary and a family friend, Jim King.

Rosemary with her parents, Rose and Albert Berkel, in Florida.

Rosemary considered wearing her sisters' hand-me-downs a badge of honor. And, 'I remember my mother sewing some,' said Rosemary, here dressed for cold weather.

Rosemary Berkel as a young Girl Scout. Scouting continued to be important to Rosemary, who was a scout leader and camp nurse later in life.

just sit around the table and talk. We didn't get up and run around. There was always something new and intriguing that they had to say that I was interested in. I learned a lot about what was going on during that time."

When playtime came, the youngsters engaged in a spirited game of badminton, or perhaps hide and seek, and as afternoon turned to evening, the games of choice became flashlight tag or kick the can under a nearby street light.

Although Rosemary remembered herself being quite competitive, it wasn't in her nature to cheat.

"I have always tried to be very honest; I always had this conscience about me. I am sure that sometimes when we were playing I did push the limits. But if I told a lie, it would worry me to death until I had to confess to Mother

or somebody and get it off my chest. So I tried to be very truthful. Lying would never be tolerated in our family."

There were chores, of course; beds had to be made every morning, and the entire house had to be tackled on the weekends — waste cans emptied, windows washed, floors swept and furniture dusted. Rosemary enjoyed most – but not all – of her responsibilities. There was no indoor plumbing, and, because rank has its privileges, she was stuck with one particularly distasteful job.

"One of my jobs as a young girl was to empty what they called the slop jar. It was a potty that we would use at night. We would keep it in the house and then anybody that had to go to the bathroom would use that, until the next morning when I would take that darn pot out to the outhouse. That wasn't the most pleasant job I have ever

Rosemary also was a majorette at Marion High School.

Albert and Rose Berkel, Rosemary's parents.

had in my life. But I was low man on the totem pole at that time."

Rosemary prided herself on being obedient, but she has no doubt there were times when she tried to get out of that job; certainly if Rosemary was sick, it fell to another of the children. Otherwise, "No, I never got by with too much. I had a pretty smart Mother."

"As far as my relationship with my parents, I loved them. Like most kids, you just accepted them. My mother was an awfully good cook. My dad was a hard worker, but he wasn't a big talker. He wasn't the type to hug you a lot until we got older. That was just the way he was raised."

Rosemary (right) and her siblings: Delores, sitting next to Rosemary; and Patricia Pulley and Jim Berkel.

As a welder, Albert's hands would get dark, particularly around his nails and in the creases of his fingers. That worried his youngest child.

"I remember, as a little girl, I would look at my hands and look at Dad's hands and wonder if his hands would ever clean up again, if he would wash them and if they would ever be like mine. He would just say that he couldn't get the grit off his hands. Sometimes, right after work, you could smell the oil or whatever he was working with. But later in life, after he had retired, I was delighted to see that he had normal hands just like mine, where all of that grit finally got off his hands, and they looked like other men's hands. As a child, that kind of worried me."

Like any youngster, Rosemary had her own superstitions and fears. She remembered instances when she would look to her dad for reassurance. When she asked Albert whether it was true that walking under a ladder was bad luck, he would respond, "Well, it is bad luck if it falls on you."

Other times, Rosemary's worries took on a more sinister tone.

"I remember another time when I was kind of tormented by something, I must have heard about somebody being kidnapped. It really stuck in my mind; for some reason, I got this fear that I was going to be kidnapped, and I didn't know how I could keep from being kidnapped.

"I remember my dad was working with his carpentry stuff, and I started talking to him about it; I said, 'Dad, something's bothering me,' and I told him about being afraid I might be kidnapped. I didn't know how to quit being so frightened. He looked at me, and he laughed. He said, 'Honey, if somebody kidnapped you at night, when they see you in the morning, they'll let you go.' Of course, I laughed too, and it turned the whole feeling around. Then he reassured me. 'No, we watch you and protect you, and nothing is going to happen. Just don't worry about anything happening to you.' Every so often, I do remember him with that sense of humor."

Rosemary vividly recalled how her dad wanted to help her with a loose tooth. She did not see any humor in his solution.

"My dad wanted to pull it, and I didn't want him to put his fingers in my mouth and pull my tooth, so he had another idea. He put a string around my tooth and then put it on a door that was ajar, then he shut the door, and it pulled my tooth right out. Of course, it scared me, and there was a little blood, and I thought I was going to die. Somehow, I did survive that," she said, smiling.

While there weren't vacations or camping trips, family and friends enjoyed being together at home, in the neighborhood and nearby.

"In the summer months, we would go to Crab Orchard Lake and up near the Carterville and Carbondale area. We would take picnic lunches, and we would go swimming in the lake. Quite frequently, we would take blankets to stretch out and take a nap in the afternoon. Just a lazy Sunday afternoon. We would either have watermelon or fried chicken or different things like that, a potluck. Whoever came would bring a dish. Somehow it would all work out."

Rosemary attended Lincoln School in Marion for first grade, but the family's move north of town put her in the Logan School District. She remembered being "pretty good" at spelling and math in grade school, no doubt because as that personality test years later would show, she had drive.

"In elementary school, we were assigned seats. I always

Rosemary Berkel loved being a majorette at Marion Junior High School.

liked to be up near the front because there were fewer distractions. When I was in the back, I was always watching what everyone else was doing in front of me. So I really liked to sit up near the front."

She clearly remembered feeling a strong sense of compassion for a girl in her class.

"I never thought about my family not having money, but I knew this girl was from a very poor family. She would come to school sometimes, and I know that she hadn't been taught or helped to bathe. A lot of people, different ones, would make fun of her. I always felt so sorry and so sad for her because I felt like it wasn't her fault. She needed help, and she wasn't getting it. That really bothered me."

Logan School also was where Rosemary was introduced to Girl Scouts, which she loved. "The mission was pretty basically as it is today – to show leadership, to teach girls high moral standards, to learn teamwork and to cooperate with their leaders and those they worked with." She later become a Girl Scout leader and was proud of being a lifelong Girl Scout.

Rosemary also discovered her passion for art in elementary school.

"I discovered that I really liked art. That just seemed to open new doors to me. Later on in life, I took classes as an amateur artist. I enjoyed acrylics and oils and colored pencils."

Her favorite teacher from elementary school through junior high was Mr. Gay.

"He was handsome. I remember in junior high — that was about the time that I was a pre-teen — and I remember standing in the lunch room line, and it was hot in there, and I passed out. He happened to be the teacher who was watching everybody, and he caught me. When I came to, I was in his arms. I remember thinking, 'Oh, my goodness.' I got teased for months afterward about that."

Rosemary also found that she enjoyed being a baton twirler. "In the eighth-grade year, I was head drum majorette. I remember we had white uniforms, and it was very military like, with white long trousers, a white jacket with a braid at the shoulder and I had a real tall white, furry hat that I wore as head drum majorette.

"I was always very excited before parades and things like that. I enjoyed the parades, and the crowds enjoying watching the band come by. I was so happy, I just would strut."

There were other discoveries in those days.

"In junior high, I went to a party. That was the first time I learned about spin the bottle, and where it stopped the boy got to kiss you. That was a new discovery. I was bashful, and I got kissed that night."

Marion didn't have a swimming pool, and cooling off in the summer meant that kids – especially boys – rode their bicycles to old mining pits that had filled with water over the years.

"They would have to ride past our house to get there. I remember there was a young kid who was unknown to me at the time. Later on, I found out that this was the young man that I would marry, it was Harry L. I would be out in the front yard practicing my baton twirling through junior high and high school, and this was just something that they did. I guess that was the first time I ever saw him. I didn't know who he was, but I remembered him."

Rosemary described herself as "a little bit above average" as a high school student. There were no rewards for A's, and she didn't recall getting into trouble at home if she didn't obtain good grades.

"My parents just generally encouraged us to do our best, to study more, and that was one of my downfalls. I didn't have a set study time, which I think that I definitely would have benefited if I had to sit down and study at a set time each night. I wasn't disciplined enough at that age to make myself do that. I wasn't taught to be disciplined. I could have done a lot better, looking back."

But Rosemary wasn't a "bad" student. She didn't get into trouble, never was suspended. Neither did she ever cheat on a test. And while she said she probably flunked a test in high school, she never flunked a course.

In addition to twirling, favorite high school activities included pep club and 4H, where Rosemary learned to sew, to make dresses, do demonstrations and talk about flower arranging and other crafts. She also belonged to a religious youth group that met at the church every Wednesday night.

Rosemary in an early formal portrait.

The popular singers of the day were also Rosemary's favorites – Perry Como, Frank Sinatra, Johnny Mathis and Andy Williams. High school girls wore blouses and skirts with wide belts, or sweaters with slacks. She was busy, had good friends and a warm, loving home. Being popular wasn't particularly important during high school days.

"I was comfortable being me. I had three older siblings telling me what to do. I was used to people liking what I did or not liking it; you learned to adjust. There were several of us that ran around together. Ours was the home where we'd get together, have cookouts or whatever. Mother was always open for us to have friends over. There were kids who I thought were more worldly than me. They lived in town, we lived in the country, they would hang out at Teen Town and other places. I wasn't involved in a clique. Whenever we'd all get together, I had no problem getting along with all of them."

"My family taught us honesty, integrity and good moral values. If I felt it was the right thing to do, I'd do it."

Her parents encouraged her to choose her friends carefully. She remembers her mother sharing two bits of wisdom with her during senior year: "Choose a date who would make a good mate, because you never know when you'll fall in love," and, "Having conflict between your head and heart, listen to the part that has brains."

When it came to dates, however, it was Rosemary's brother who ran unwelcome interference for his little sister. "With one year and one day difference in our age, he knew all the guys I knew. Guys who wanted to go out with me my junior or senior year, they'd talk to Jim. If he didn't like them, he'd say, 'No, she can't go out with you.' I found this out by chance, and I wasn't too happy. I told him, 'Let me make my own choices.'"

If there was anything that she wished might have been different, Rosemary would say it was her looks.

"I never felt I was very attractive. There were girls who seemed like they had such natural beauty and poise. I never felt I quite had that, especially outside beauty. I learned it's what comes from the heart, what's inside that

matters. I never really felt jealous that somebody else got on homecoming court. It would have been nice if I had the looks and the popularity, but I was always glad for those who got that."

Though he appreciates her humility, Ray Hancock disagrees with her self-assessment. He and Rosemary were friends since they attended Washington Junior High School in Marion together.

"In high school, she was very pretty, extremely personable. She liked almost everybody, and almost everybody liked her. She came from a very humble background, so it was all very natural, and it was not feigned in any way. She was very sociable, as well; she participated in all the little parties we had, athletic events. She and I were kind of in the same neighborhood. She was always special, a little prettier than most girls, a little bit more sociable than most girls."

He pointed out, "Not many of us who come from humble backgrounds have big egos. We all have different personalities, but Rosemary and I were a little bit alike in those ways. We both liked to have good fun and laugh and be on the humorous side."

What mattered most was that as she began to mature, Rosemary "learned who she was. She began to learn, like many of us. We learned who we were, and we learned it was as good as other people and maybe better, so the confidence began to grow," Ray recalls. "By the time Rosemary was a freshman or sophomore in high school, she was a different person. She was more confident, more outgoing, such as her being a drum majorette. She became one of the more popular girls in school, one of the leaders in her class in all the activities we had. She had a lot of opportunities for boyfriends, she was sociable. By her junior and senior years, she really blossomed into a beautiful woman with a great personality."

As the end of her high schools days approached, Rosemary concluded – not surprisingly – that she wanted a future where her focus would be on serving others. As it turned out, in her heart, she had known since junior high exa.·tly where that career path would lead.

A Commitment to Caring

Rosemary, a nursing graduate, was proud to have R.N. — Registered Nurse — behind her name, as well as wearing the uniform and cap.

'We are here to add what we can to life,
not to get what we can from life.'

– Dr. William Osler, Canadian physician

*W*hen it came to Rosemary's commitment to nursing and health care – particularly women's health – no truer words ever were spoken than those of Dr. William Osler.

A Marion family for whom she babysat while in junior high served as her first inspiration.

"Our Catholic priest was a good friend of Howard and Evelyn Dibble. Dr. Dibble had been working at the VA Hospital, and he was going to go into private practice as a surgeon. When he set up his office, his wife Evvie, who was a registered nurse, became his office nurse. They needed a babysitter for their three children. So, Father suggested me, they interviewed me, and I was hired. I worked for several years for them. Seeing Evvie Dibble in that crisp, white uniform and watching her go to the office and being enthused about it, that stimulated my interest in nursing."

In high school, with two sisters working as secretaries, Rosemary assumed, "That's what I would be." But one day, as she was learning typing and shorthand, she realized that was not the future she dreamed of. She told her teacher of her wish to pursue nursing and was allowed to take biology, chemistry and other related classes. As graduation approached, she was focused on nursing schools.

"Dr. Dibble was the one who helped me choose two Catholic schools, one in St. Louis, and I did not get in there," Rosemary said. "I went to St. Mary's in Evansville, Ind. And I was really happy. It was a smaller school. There were 54 who graduated in my class, I think. I really am very proud of that school. It is no longer open now; they went with the University of Evansville."

The family paid for her schooling with a scholarship loan provided by Giles Electric, where her dad worked as a welder. The goal was to get more nurses to return to Marion, so

Rosemary Berkel, R.N.

St. Mary's Hospital

School of Nursing

Class of 1958

Rosemary (second row, third from left) was in St. Mary's Hospital School of Nursing class of 1958 in Evansville, Ind.

when Rosemary came back to work at Marion Memorial Hospital, paycheck deductions repaid her loan. That money, in turn, helped someone else receive a scholarship.

Rosemary earned her three-year nursing degree from St. Mary's Hospital School of Nursing, but she had to overcome some early struggles.

"As a freshman in nurse's training, you don't know exactly what you're getting into. School was difficult; there's so much material you have to learn. I wondered, as most of us did, 'Will I be able to make it through here?'"

Also, during her first six weeks in Evansville, Rosemary found herself terribly homesick.

"I remember going to Sister Catherine, our director, telling her I felt like crying because I so missed home. I will never forget, she was wearing the coronet hat with the point at the top, and she leaned back in her chair, laughing. And here I was heart-broken because I was so homesick.

"She said, 'Miss Berkel, do you know how lucky you are to have such a close-knit family that you miss so much? There are so many people out there who don't have a close-knit family like that. This is a special blessing. If you really think you want to be a nurse, I want you to know that it's OK to cry if you feel like it, then go do something else. I think you'll make a good nurse and don't give it up yet.'"

Sister Catherine gave Rosemary exactly the boost in confidence she needed at that moment.

"It really deeply touched me, and after that I didn't feel like I had to cry so much," Rosemary said. "I was 19 years old at that time. I'm glad I stuck to my nursing. I've always loved nursing."

Like all students, she preferred certain classes over others.

"I loved anatomy, especially when we dissected animals," she said. "In nursing school, we would go down to the morgue, and we'd be able to see the doctor who would try to find out what caused a patient to die."

"As we progressed in nurse's training, going into my senior year, it was exciting to get that far. A lot of girls who started with us in freshman year didn't make it. I made it because I worked hard. When I really focused and studied, that just opened new thought processes."

Nursing school presented opportunities for Rosemary and her classmates to experience various specializations.

"I went to Indianapolis to a tuberculosis sanitarium for six weeks. I also went to St. Louis for three months at St. Vincent de Paul, where they had mental patients. I did learn that wasn't the kind of nursing I wanted to be involved in. I also went to Louisville for three months for pediatrics."

Her goal throughout that period? "To get through nurse's training and come back to Marion Memorial and work as a nurse. I have always loved taking care of people."

Rosemary recalled the "very intense" testing for the state boards. After completing the testing in Indianapolis, Ind., she returned to Marion.

"I remember receiving in the mail the letter saying whether I had passed my state boards or not and what an exciting day – I passed it on the first testing. And I can remember going around all day saying, 'I'm a registered nurse, I made it, I'm a registered nurse.' I felt so proud to have that accomplishment."

She worked as a staff nurse in the medical-surgical unit of Marion Memorial Hospital in 1958 and 1959.

"I realized that there were some patients who we could help and some patients would be terminal with their illness. But I had also been taught that we could help them bridge that gap from this life into the next, too, and help to ease their pain and anxiety. And this gave me a lot of self-satisfaction."

Later, Rosemary was offered a night supervisor position, which she accepted. She remained in the job until she married Harry L. in 1960, when they agreed she would stay at home. Rosemary still volunteered her time as a private nurse for friends and relatives.

She also continued to provide her dedicated service and expertise at the local, state and national levels. She maintained professional designations with the American Nurses Association, Illinois Nurses Association and 14th District Nurses Association.

From 1970 to 1985, Rosemary served as a volunteer nurse for the Red Cross blood mobile and was a volunteer Girl Scout camp nurse.

She spent a year, 1997 to 1998, as a member of the Illinois Women's Health Campaign Planning Team, appointed by then-Illinois First Lady Brenda Edgar because of Rosemary's efforts on behalf of women's health in Southern Illinois and her nursing background. Rosemary, she says, "was such a beautiful representative of that part of the state."

Between 1996 and 2002, she belonged to the Washington, D.C.-based Society for Advancement of Women's Health Research; and from 1998 to 2007, she served on the board of directors of the Hands of Hope Family Clinic, a free clinic in Marion.

Her commitment to her profession earned her appointments to prominent national organizations. In 2003, Tommy Thompson, then-secretary of the U.S. Department of Health and Human Services, appointed Rosemary to a three-year term on the National Institutes of Health's National Advisory Council for Nursing Research, based in Washington, D.C. Between 1987 and 1994, she was a member of the National League for Nursing-CHAP (Community Health Accreditation Program) Board of Governors, based in New York City.

It was her compassion and her love of taking care of others that prompted Rosemary to remain so active in nursing and health issues throughout her life. She derived satisfaction from continuing to learn and sharing her knowledge with others. And while collecting honors and accolades for her efforts was not her goal, she earned many.

In 1991, the National League for Nursing presented Rosemary with its Anna M. Filmore Award "for outstanding contributions in developing and administering community health services."

In her acceptance speech, Rosemary talked about the "doors of opportunity" that nursing offers.

"I specifically recall Miss Mabel McCracken, one of my instructors in nurse's training, who devoted her entire life to nursing. She stood before our class, the epitome of the profession in her crisp, starched uniform, and addressed us. She said, 'Ladies, nursing is your passport to the world!'

"I have never forgotten that statement. Nursing has opened many doors for me. I've had the opportunity to tour hospitals in the U.S. and travel internationally to countries such as Japan. My husband and I accompanied the governor of Illinois on a tour of the health-care facilities, pharmaceutical companies, and met with leaders in the medical profession in Israel. In addition, we observed children's day-care centers interacting with long-term nursing care facilities in Copenhagen, Denmark."

Rosemary, with daughter Cathy, put her skills and education to good use, serving as Girl Scout camp nurse.

Whether overseas or in her own backyard, Rosemary described her efforts in promoting health care as "truly an honor." And she challenged the nurses and other health-care professionals in the audience that day "to reach out in your communities."

"It is like a boomerang. The effort, energy and knowledge you extend will not only come back to you, but will come back two-fold."

Among her other honors were: Rosemary Berkel Crisp Hall of Nursing, Southeast Missouri State University in Cape Girardeau, 1988; The Society of Nursing Professionals Who's Who in Professional Nursing, 1990; Sigma Theta Tau International Honor Society of Nursing, 1991; Quality Service Award — Home Health Care, presented by Quality of Life Services, Inc., "for outstanding dedication and commitment to health care in Southern Illinois," 1990.

"I've never been sorry that I took the path I did with nursing," Rosemary often said. "Not only did I love it as a profession, but down the road in my life, when family and friends were ill, but also me personally, my nursing has been a wonderful thing to prepare me and help me cope during my life."

A June 14, 1973, newspaper photograph captures one of Rosemary's great loves: Nursing. The original caption reads 'Bug bites and bruises and other minor mishaps are well taken care of at the camp site first aid tent. Head nurse Mrs. Rosemary Crisp treats Mary Pat Dingrando as Carole and Lee Crisp supervise the act.'

Best Friends

Rosemary and Harry L. enjoyed spending time together, and were a loving couple. 'We've always been very touchy people, very lovable, very affectionate,' Rosemary said.

'All romance is grounded on friendship.'
— Henry David Thoreau

*R*osemary and Harry L.'s nearly 48-year love story didn't exactly start out like a fairy tale.

Even Harry L. admits, "She was very unimpressed with this arrogant, cocky former Marine."

It was March 1959, and 22-year-old Rosemary, fresh out of St. Mary's Hospital School of Nursing in Evansville, Ind., was living her dream and working as a nurse at Marion Memorial Hospital. Likewise, Harry L., just out of the Marine Corps, had returned to his beloved Marion and was in the profession that he loved, working for Pepsi. He also belonged to the Marion Junior Chamber of Commerce.

A Miss Marion beauty pageant was approaching, and several friends persuaded Rosemary – "for the lack of them having contestants" she would say with her trademark humility – to enter the pageant.

"The night of the pageant, they had men from the Junior Chamber of Commerce as escorts," Rosemary recalled. "Harry L. was backstage, and I noticed him flirting with all the girls, and I was really not very impressed."

That was of little concern to Harry L. "At about 22 years old, I was noticing a lot of girls at that time."

Rosemary was dating a gentleman named Bob from Notre Dame who lived in Evansville, and he was in the audience that night. "He was Catholic, my mother liked him, and she thought we had a bright future."

Backstage before the pageant, "Harry L. came over and started kind of flirting with me. But, if I went with a guy, I went with a guy, and I didn't flirt around with others. I

Rosemary and Harry L. in the pool at Crisp Acres in Marion.

know that sounds boring. He said, 'Well, I guess you have a boyfriend.' And I said, 'Yes, I do.' And he said, 'Well, is he here?' and I said 'Yes, he is.' And I thought, maybe this'll get this guy off my back.

"He said, 'Well, let me see him.' We opened the drapes and Harry L. saw him. Bob was kind of tall, with a blond-headed business haircut and horn-rimmed glasses. He did look like a businessman. Harry L. looked at him, closed the drapes, turned around and looked at me and said, 'Can't you do better than that?'

Rosemary Berkel (third from right) was a candidate in the Miss Marion beauty pageant in 1959.

"And I thought, 'This egotistical guy.' This was really a turn-off for me. So I didn't think a thing about him after that."

The same can't be said for Harry L. Today, he chuckles at the memory of that first encounter. "I'm a salesman. You first have to get their attention. There's the approach, the presentation and the close."

Rosemary's good friend, Carol Chamness, won the pageant. All the participants were told they would be invited to attend a future beauty pageant in Mt. Vernon, Ill., and that a Jaycee member would call and take the ladies to the event.

Rosemary got a call from Harry L., who told her he was going to take her to the Mt. Vernon pageant.

"He came by to pick me up and on our way to Mt. Vernon, I said, 'Aren't you picking someone else up?' He said, 'No, you're the only one they assigned me to.' Of course, that's what he had lined up." She rolled her eyes as she recalled the exchange. "I turned and I looked at him and I said, 'Now remember, this isn't a date.' I'm one of these people who was trying to do it right. My mother and father taught me well, I guess."

For Rosemary that evening, Harry L. was merely her escort. He viewed things a bit differently.

"On the way home, I'll never forget. He pulled over, and he wanted to park with me. And I remember saying to him, 'You know, if that's what you are interested in, I am not and just please take me home.'"

What she couldn't have known at the time was that she was getting an introduction to Harry L.'s persistence and determination. At the same time, she was beginning to question her relationship with Bob. A special dance

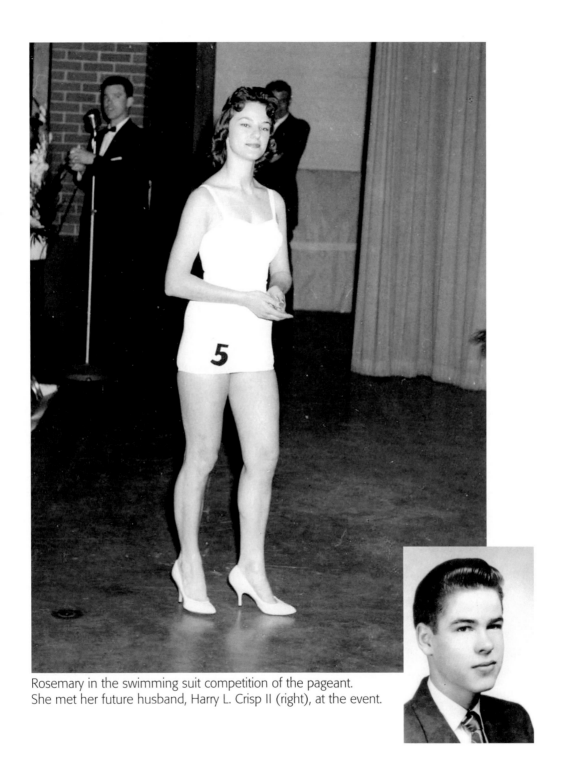

Rosemary in the swimming suit competition of the pageant.
She met her future husband, Harry L. Crisp II (right), at the event.

Harry L. Crisp II attended Culver Military Academy in Culver, Ind., and later served in the U.S. Marine Corps.

went to in Evansville turned out to be a defining moment for Rosemary. Rosemary was not at all pleased with how the evening transpired.

"This was when I knew it wasn't going to work out."

Bob had previously given Rosemary a miniature of his fraternity ring. Once she decided she didn't want to see him anymore, she sent the ring back to him.

"Afterwards, he sent me a note saying how sorry he was, with a red rose. My mother thought that was so sweet and that maybe I should think this thing over again. But there was nothing special there."

That episode provided Harry L. with exactly the opening he needed.

"Somehow, somebody let him know that Bob and I had broken it off. Harry L. called, looking to start all over again." And that they did.

Candidates For Queen of Military Ball
[First Of A Series]

MISS MARJORIE JEAN SAUNDERS, Quincy, Ill., sponsored by Pershing Rifles; Quincy Senior High School.

MISS ROSE MARY BERKEL, Marion, Ill., sponsored by Newman Club; college, St. Mary's School of Nursing, Evansville, Ind.

Rosemary (right) was a candidate for Queen of the Military Ball at Rolla, Mo., in 1956.

Before renewing their acquaintance, however, Rosemary had accepted a position as head nurse at a summer camp in Singer, Wis.

"We had dated up until that time, and I was wondering if I really wanted to go be a camp nurse."

At that point, they had been dating for about three months. But, she had an obligation to fulfill. Within a week of arriving at camp, Rosemary started getting phone calls from Harry L.

"When you got phone calls or made phone calls, you had to go all the way up the hill to the camp caretaker's house," she said. "It was fine for a while with the caretaker, but then the calls became more prevalent." There was that persistence again.

53

Finally, Harry L. headed to Wisconsin to visit Rosemary at the camp for a long weekend.

"It took him three airplanes to get up there," she recalled, laughing. "He proposed to me when he was up in Singer. I said yes, but I also said that we would wait. I didn't want to say anything about it, because I wanted him to ask my mother and father before we did anything else or let anybody else know. So, he agreed with that. And he gave me my ring in October; he proposed to me again in the car at the back of Crisp Acres."

Much had changed in a rather short period of time, particularly Harry L.'s first impression that he was flirting with "just a cute girl."

"The more I chased her, the more I found out there was a lot more to her than just the looks," he says. "She had character, she was a deep thinker, a caring person. Infatuation started to change from just that to a deeper fondness and eventually into love."

In Harry L.'s mind, their courtship was "reasonably short."

"I had probably done all the running around that I wanted to do. She was out of school and in a profession she loved, nursing. We were both back in Marion, both back in Southern Illinois. It was the right time of life."

At 10 a.m. Jan. 16, 1960, the salesman "closed" the deal. Rosemary Ann Berkel and Harry L. Crisp II were pronounced husband and wife in St. Joseph Catholic Church in Marion. Their reception was in the Knights of Columbus Hall behind the small white wooden church.

Their love for each other was enduring. They were hopeless romantics. Rosemary picked out "Stardust" as their theme song early in their marriage. She had the words "Love is eternal" inscribed in Harry L.'s wedding ring. On every special occasion, be it the birth of one of their children, a wedding anniversary or other special days, Harry L. always sent Rosemary yellow roses.

Her dad, says daughter Car... s a wonderful man. He is giving, he is smart, but ... s a tough man. Mom

A young Harry L. and Rosemary Crisp at dinner.

Rosemary's mother, Rose Berkel, adjusts the bride's veil before Rosemary's marriage to Harry L. Rosemary had paid rent to her parents while in college, which was given back to Rosemary to purchase the bridal gown.

A proud father, Albert Berkel, escorts daughter Rosemary to the altar Jan. 16, 1960.

The newlyweds pose while cutting their wedding cake.

Mr. and Mrs. Harry L. Crisp II; best man Bud Bobo is in the background.

Father Rich, Rosemary's priest at St. Joseph's parish and a close friend of the couple, describes them as 'remarkably close ... they were like high school kids.'

softened him up so much. He let her know she was so special. They'd be watching TV, or she'd be cleaning up, and he'd say to her, 'Rosemary, have I told you today how much I love you?'"

Neither were they shy about letting the world see how much they were in love. It really didn't matter where they were or what they were doing, including attending business-related dinners.

"So often at those functions, they will separate the man from the wife," Rosemary said. "And Harry L. doesn't like that because he likes for us to sit together. We're invariably holding hands under the table, on top of the table; we've done it for all the years that we've been married. I'll be sitting there, and I'll notice his leg is next to mine, touching it. We've always been very touchy people, very lovable, very affectionate."

Father Rich, Rosemary's priest at St. Joseph's parish and a dear friend to the couple, describes them as "remarkably close."

"When you think, both of them with their schedules, how many marriages don't struggle? But they were like high school kids."

Rosemary and Harry L. dance the night away.

The couple enjoy some Pepsi while boating.

Harry L. and Rosemary have lunch on vacation in Florida.

Harry L. and Rosemary share an embrace.

Rosemary counseled her daughters on the importance of finding the balance between the demands of being a mother and a wife. 'Don't forget your husband and his feelings and his emotional needs,' said Rosemary, here with Harry L.

Harry L. chauffeurs Rosemary in a golf cart during a Florida trip.

There were occasional bumps in the road, as is true in most every relationship. But they were few and far between – and brief.

"I can't remember a serious argument in our marriage on her part," Harry L. says. "Sometimes I'd get a little cantankerous. But she was a believer that we never went to sleep mad, that we needed to make up before that because if you carry those grudges, it brings baggage to the marriage. I can't remember a serious argument in our whole marriage."

Rosemary had her own methods of resolving those rare conflicts.

"No. 1, when one person has gotten mad and lost their temper, it's better for the other person, rather than coming back and saying hateful things, it's better to listen to what they have to say and then to try to keep your temper down," she advised. "Wait until later on in the discussion and say, 'You know, you said some awfully hateful things to me, and it really hurt my feelings, and let's talk about it.' I think you have to be a good listener, too, because sometimes you'll think, 'Oh, it's not this way at all,' and you need to look at the way you came across. Maybe you're coming across different than you meant to be. This is something you really have to work on: when you're angry to not say the worst, harsh things. Because you'll get it out of your system but those hateful words have gone over to your partner and they are still being hurt by that. And sometimes that's not just for that day, but for days."

She also counseled her daughters on the importance of finding the balance between the demands of being a mother and a wife.

"Your baby's going to get the attention just out of necessity. Don't forget your husband and his feelings and his emotional needs. There's a special bond for mothers and their babies, and you just automatically give a lot of time and attention. But when you are with your husband, and the baby has quieted down, try to eat with him, give some time to him in particular. As the kids grew older, I had set a bed time of about 8 o'clock, especially during the school year, not only so they could get their rest, but that also gives you quality time to be with your husband, and I think that's so important."

Harry L. was Rosemary's knight in shining armor, the one to whom she would turn whenever she had a problem.

"He would always come to my rescue."

Harry L. readily acknowledges what a lucky man he has been.

"God blessed me so much. When you marry someone, you don't know these things. She was such a good person. For several years, I couldn't believe it. I wondered, 'Is this a front, what is she doing?' It was the real thing. God looked after me, because I wasn't that smart to figure it out when I met her."

Knowing that his wife would be thrilled, Harry L. converted to Catholicism on what would have been their 48th wedding anniversary.

"She always encouraged me to become Catholic. I always went to the Catholic church, even though when we first married I was a deacon in the First Christian Church. But I committed to raising the kids Catholic when we married, and I certainly didn't want to confuse the issue by me going to one church and the family going to another. So I always went to the Catholic church. She always encouraged me to convert, and it was one of her big failures in life not getting me to become a Catholic. I fulfilled that because I felt it would please her."

Rosemary no doubt smiled down at Harry L. on that day, just as she continues to smile down on the family they raised and their successful business enterprise.

Harry L. and Rosemary were married nearly 48 years. 'I can't remember a serious argument in our marriage on her part,' Harry L. says. 'She was a believer that we never went to sleep mad, that we needed to make up before that ...'

Harry L. and Rosemary are ready for a bike ride on Father's Day 2004.

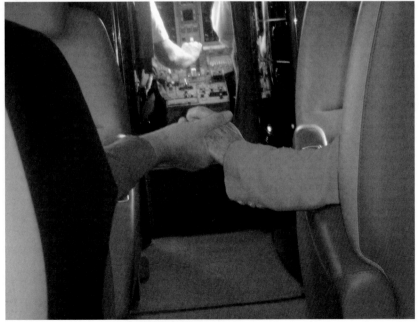

Holding hands was one of the many ways Rosemary and Harry L. showed their affection for one another.

Rosemary waves to her family as she and Harry L. head out for yet another adventure.

Rosemary and Harry L. wave from their dinghy, off the coast of Florida in Key Largo.

Rosemary and Harry L. pause during a tour of the Rosemary Berkel and Harry L. Crisp II Southeast Regional Museum on the campus of Southeast Missouri State University in Cape Girardeau. It was one of Rosemary's last public appearances, in the fall of 2007. She was determined to see the building and walked all around it, even though she had to stop several times to rest.

A portrait of Harry L. and Rosemary captures their contentment. In was painted in 1983 by Jean Heath, wife of Heath Candy Co. president Bob Heath.

Growing Family Growing Business

A 1992 Crisp family portrait: Cathy and Cara (front); Cyndi, Cheryl and Carole; Harry 'Lee,' Rosemary and Harry L.

'A house without children
is like a garden without flowers.'

— Tunisian proverb

The newlyweds' first home was a three-bedroom rental, and it met their needs for only two years. Rosemary and Harry L. welcomed their first child, Cyndi, into the world in the early fall of 1960.

"I had delivered many babies in my role as a nurse. I had delivered three on my own when the doctor couldn't make it. But when you have children of your own, it's an awesome responsibility. You take each day at a time. It's a different learning process."

After being a registered nurse, Rosemary made the decision to be a stay-at-home mom. As she was adjusting to life with a newborn, Harry L. was busy providing for his new family.

"I could have told you at any age that, one, I wanted to live in Marion, Illinois; two, that I wanted to be in the Pepsi business; and three, that I wanted to eventually be successful and have a pretty good-sized business," he says. "And I could have told you all of that probably at 10 years old. I have not deviated from that."

Harry L. hung around his dad's Pepsi plant all the time as a kid, obviously knowing that he wanted to follow in his father's footsteps. His family, of course, had come a long

Harry L. and Harry Sr. outside the Pepsi MidAmerica plant on North Market in Marion.

Harry L. and Rosemary with daughter Cyndi in 1962.

way from the days of his dad running a poultry and egg business. As Harry L. tells the story, his dad started selling strawberry and orange soft drinks – named, appropriately, Red Rooster – from the back of those chicken trucks. A Pepsi franchise manager approached him, saying there had never been any Pepsi in the Southern Illinois market. His dad bought some bottling equipment from an RC plant in Pinckneyville that had gone out of business, and the new franchise got its start with his dad selling Pepsi from the back of those chicken trucks.

"They didn't have anything but hard work and some initiative and drive, and they were able to create a business that so many people in this area benefit from," Harry L. says.

He came by his business instincts naturally. His dad served 12 years as Marion's mayor and then decided to leave politics and get into business, which Harry L. noted, chuckling, was the first time "we made a living, so we were glad he did that." His dad was quite the entrepreneur; he built the Marion bowling alley, which was the first in the Midwest; he owned the Marion Evening Post newspaper; he owned a wooden case factory in Goreville; and he was a Borden's ice cream distributor.

"He was smart, hard-working and fortunate," Harry L. says of his dad. "We all need opportunities for things to turn out for us."

Harry L. was working in the plant when he married Rosemary. He eventually moved to the sales side of the operation, visiting its different offices and "working out in the trade."

"It all grew, as time went on. Rosemary was always in there, not only with the kids and raising a family, but she

Rosemary with daughters Cyndi, Carole, Cheryl and Cathy in 1969.

Rosemary and the girls —
Carole, Cyndi, Cathy and
Cheryl — on a Florida beach
in 1968.

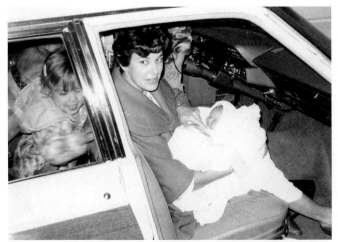

Rosemary brings home Carole in 1966; Cheryl is in the back.

Harry 'Lee' Crisp III with his mother.

was full of character and integrity. She was very devout religiously. She loved church and God and her family. She loved life."

The couple faced their first significant challenge in 1961, when Rosemary suffered a miscarriage while three months pregnant.

"That was very difficult for me. By three months, you know that you're pregnant. But I got through it with a lot of love and support."

Cathy was born in 1962. "That was very special," Rosemary said of the birth of their second daughter. That same year the family moved into the house they built on Suzanne Drive. They had purchased the lot before they married. The childhood home for all of the children has remained in the family for 48 years; their son, Lee, and his family live there now.

Having lived by the philosophy that if they couldn't afford something, they wouldn't buy it, Harry L. found himself having to grit his teeth now with a house payment.

"The only money we borrowed was when we built our first house. That was the toughest $350 of my life every month making that house payment. After 10 years, we got that paid off, and that was a good celebration for both of us. We believed in living beneath our means financially, and we always did so."

Though she had a newborn and a toddler, Rosemary kept a neat home and looked forward each day to her husband's return from his busy work day.

"My mother always said, 'Before your husband comes home, be sure that you freshen up, comb your hair, put fresh makeup on and greet your husband. Remember, he's going to be out in public with a lot of different people.' I've carried that throughout life."

Rosemary found herself truly tested after the couple's third child, Cheryl, was born in 1964.

"We had Cyndi, who was 4, Cathy, who wasn't quite 2, and then I had Cheryl. She was a preemie — 4 pounds, 12 ounces — and she arrived in the middle of the night. Her lungs didn't fully inflate. This was a very difficult time; I was in the hospital for about five days. For about three of those days, her lungs were having difficulty inflating. It was a few years after

W.W. 'Foots' Clements of Dr Pepper (left) with Cyndi, Cathy, Cheryl, Carole, Cara, Rosemary, Harry 'Lee,' Violette (Harry L.'s mother) and Harry L. at the Pepsi MidAmerica Christmas party.

The family poses for a Christmas card photo: (seated on the floor) Cathy, Cheryl, Cyndi and Carole; Rosemary, Cara, Harry L. and Harry 'Lee.'

Harry Sr. gives a golf-cart ride to Rosemary and Carole (in passenger seat) and (clockwise from left) Cathy, Cheryl, Harry L. and Cyndi.

Harry L. and Rosemary in the summer of 1966 with Cathy, Cyndi and Cheryl.

Harry L. at work in his office at Pepsi MidAmerica.

Rosemary looks out for daughters Cheryl, Cathy and Cyndi at the pool at Crisp Acres. Carole was born a few months later.

It was 1965, and the family was dressed for Easter: Harry L., Cathy, Cyndi, Cheryl and Rosemary.

Dad, Mom and daughters Carole, Cheryl, Cyndi and Cathy at the 1969 grand opening of Pepsi MidAmerica. Harry 'Lee' joined the family a few months later.

Rosemary and her daughters greet guests at the grand opening.

Breaking ground for a Pepsi MidAmerica expansion of the administration building in mid-1980s are Harry L. and Rosemary Crisp, then Illinois Gov. James Thompson and Marion Mayor Bob Butler.

Actress Joan Crawford helps pop the top of a replica of a Pepsi bottle at the grand opening in 1969 of Pepsi MidAmerica's current location. Joining her on the podium were (from left) Jim Summerall, president of Pepsi, Harry L. and Harry Sr.

Breaking ground for Crisp Container in 1996 are (from left) president of Crown Cork and Seal Bill Avery, Crisp grandsons Cameron and Tyler Newbold, Rosemary, Harry L., Illinois Gov. Jim Edgar, Marion city commissioner Robert 'Dog' Connell, Rep. Larry Woolard, Father Richard Mohr and Marion Mayor Bob Butler.

Rosemary, who had just received her Inspiring Women award in October 2007, is photographed with her family: (Front row) Carole Schwarm, Cara Sims, Rosemary, Cheryl Rabbitt; (back row) Stacie and Harry 'Lee,' Mark Schwarm, Chris Sims, Harry L., Bob Rabbitt, Greg Wilson (a family friend) and Cathy Newbold.

The December 1970 Christmas card: Harry L. holding Harry 'Lee'; (clockwise from top) Rosemary, Cathy, Cheryl, Carole and Cyndi.

Harry L. and Rosemary with President George W. Bush
and First Lady Laura Bush.

Harry L. and Rosemary
with President Ronald Reagan.

President Kennedy's baby died, and that was in my mind.," Rosemary said, referring to the Kennedys' infant son, Patrick Bouvier Kennedy, who died two days after birth.

Members of the hospital staff would take Cheryl out of the nursery to get X-rays, only to see her turning blue and rushing to get her back on oxygen. Daughter number three, Rosemary said, "was a strong-willed child, and she finally survived it. I was a nursing mother, and that helped us through it."

Finally able to return home, it wasn't long before Rosemary found herself confronting a whole new set of unexpected challenges.

"When I came home, I realized I had had a hand for each child. When I had a third one, it seemed overwhelming. Cheryl had her days and nights mixed up, she was awake most of the night, and the other two had day routines. I wasn't getting much sleep, and I got worn down. I went to the doctor, and he put me on a high-potency vitamin. I felt depressed; it was more than I could handle. The laundry was building up. It was difficult to get meals on the table. Of course, I had to nurse the baby every couple of hours. It was a very, very difficult time for me, and, of course, the other children needed attention too."

While they hadn't been able to afford help at home in the early days of their marriage, that had changed by the time Cheryl was born. While Harry L. tried to persuade his wife that they should hire a housekeeper, Rosemary wouldn't hear any of it.

"I felt I was a super mom. My mother never had help, my two sisters didn't, 'I ought to be able to do this.' I wouldn't do it. But I learned quickly that I had no choice. I got so down. One afternoon, it was quiet, and I wanted to lie down for a bit. I was kneeling down beside my bed, feeling that I had reached rock-bottom. And I said, 'Dear God, I cannot do this by myself. If you will be my co-pilot through life, you and I will be able to face anything.' Through life, I had always put my life in God's hands, and I have ever since, and this is what helped me to survive those times."

Rosemary hired her cousin, Bonnie Berkel, to help with the house. The family welcomed daughter number four,

Carole, into the world in 1966. Sadly, another difficult challenge would follow.

"I had miscarried within a year after Carole was born," Rosemary recalled. "I always felt like this was the way God took care of something that was not going to be normal and healthy. But, I feel like someday when I get to heaven, I'm going to get to see those babies."

The family continued to grow, with the birth of Harry Lee Crisp III – Lee – in 1970 and then Cara in 1973. Somehow, Rosemary always managed to balance the demands of motherhood with those of supporting her husband, all of which she did gracefully.

"She always took the approach that I came first, my work was very important to us," Harry L. says. "I always knew that if I took care of business, it would take care of us. At the drop of a hat, she would go with me to meetings or dinners, even though she may have prepared dinner for the entire family. She did whatever it took. I can't say enough of how supportive she always was. Still, neither one of us ever neglected the children. We had priorities to accomplish some good things for our family."

It was very much a two-way street. Getting the kids to Mass, while a rather significant undertaking with six of them, was an important part of the upbringing the couple provided. Rosemary, just like her mom did with her four children, made sure the children were dressed appropriately for church, including bows in all the girls' hair. One Sunday, in the rush to get the kids ready and make it to Mass on time, Rosemary walked into church with her slippers on. "Well, if that's the worst thing I ever do, that's not so bad."

"I would always take all six kids," Rosemary said. "When I was pregnant or just getting over having babies, Harry L. always made sure the children were taken to Mass or for their catechism class. He was very supportive of the Catholic faith and very supportive of raising our kids Catholic."

Rosemary loved being a stay-at-home mom. That meant she could help them get their day started and be there to learn all about it when they returned home. As she would say years later, "I was like a kid doing things with them."

Holidays, birthdays — she loved them all and made each one special. For Valentine's Day, Rosemary made a red

The 1979 Christmas card: (Seated) Cara, Harry L., Rosemary, Harry 'Lee'; (standing) Cyndi, Cathy, Cheryl and Carole.

cake and had a little heart-shaped box of chocolates at each of the children's breakfast plate. It would be the first thing that would greet them on Valentine's mornings. Birthdays were slumber parties and theme parties – and always memorable.

There also were moments that are etched in memory because of how frightening they were at the time.

One evening, when Lee was about 2 1/2 years old, Rosemary fed him dinner and put him to bed. She was about to pour out what was left in his cup of milk as she did the dishes, but instead decided to take the cup into the bedroom to see if Lee wanted to finish it.

"My guardian angel must have been taking care of us, because I went in there – and I had had four daughters prior to this, same bed, same window, same roller blinds – and somehow Lee had gotten a hold of the blind, he had reached up and got hold of the string, got it down and somehow got it over his head. When I went in there, a few more minutes, and he would have been dead. He was hanging by his head, he was bowed down, he was limp."

Dressed in a robe and pregnant with Cara, Rosemary rushed to Harry L. with Lee, who was breathing, and told her husband what happened. Their next-door neighbor was Dr. Morgan, so Harry L. grabbed Lee from Rosemary and rushed him next door. Dr. Morgan kept an eye on Lee for a couple of hours and warned the couple that because it was unclear how long the flow of oxygen to Lee's brain might have been cut off, he could have brain damage. Fortunately, that wasn't the case.

Then there's the story of 1 1/2-year-old Cara surviving a fall out of the family camper during a stop on a trip to Florida. The fall broke her collarbone, knocked her out, and she stopped breathing. While Rosemary administered CPR, Harry L. rushed to a nearby police officer for help. With Rosemary in the front seat of the squad car tending to Cara and Harry L. in back, the officer took the fastest route to the closest hospital – which meant going up an exit ramp onto the interstate.

"Just before we got to the emergency room, Cara started moving around, she was moving her head, and as soon as I saw that, I knew she was going to be OK," Rosemary recalled.

Another incident involving Cara always made Rosemary smile. Her youngest child was in first grade, and one day after school, Cara demanded confirmation that she had been adopted. She was the only one of the Crisp children with white blonde hair, bright blue eyes and freckles, and she told her mom, "Everybody else says I don't look like anybody else in the family. Just tell me I'm adopted."

Once Rosemary was able to calm her daughter down, she learned that Cara got the idea from a little boy in her class who had been adopted and had been talking about it at school that day. After thinking about it for the entire school day, poor Cara, Rosemary recalled, laughing, was "hot under the collar" by the time she got home.

Harry L. always made sure there was a special time, regularly, with each of his children.

"He wanted quality time with the kids, and so what he would do is invite each child on different days to go out to breakfast with him," Rosemary recalled. "Sometimes, the kids would complain because he was so well-known in our community, there's always somebody stopping by to talk or they'd sit down to eat, and the kids were like, 'We're having to share our dad with this person.' It was a wonderful experience for him to take the kids like that, and he did it quite frequently."

With their large household, it's no surprise there were expectations of the kids, and structure.

"Harry L. and I have been strict parents," Rosemary said. "We believe in them going to church and having jobs around the house. As they were growing up, one would be responsible for setting the table at night. They were responsible for making their beds. They always had to lay their clothes out the night before. We had to have organization, or we'd never make it to school on time."

Along with organization, communication was key in that big household. The family shared dinner every night. And there was a family conference at least every two weeks, once a week whenever possible.

"We'd all sit around, and one of the rules was, we'd open it for discussion, and if there were things that were bothering someone in the family, and they wanted to be somewhat critical, that was fine," Rosemary explained. "But we also insisted that the same ones found something

Harry 'Lee' plays Santa as his sisters and mother gather 'round. They are (clockwise from center) Cara, Rosemary, Cheryl, Cyndi, Cathy and Carole.

to be positive about in our family. It was good. In families, you always have these irritating things that happen along the way, and there's a lot of give and take. I think the kids will think back that it was beneficial for us."

Harry L. took over the business after a third heart attack took his dad's life in 1975. For all of his hard work, sacrifice and devotion to his profession, Harry L. never hesitates to give his wife credit for the role she played in the success of Pepsi MidAmerica.

"She was like the Rock of Gibraltar, always providing encouragement. I remember when I was calling on SIU, she was pregnant, and none of our products were being sold there. We'd go to basketball games in the old Davies Gym and sit on those bleachers. I didn't know who to call on at SIU. I was trying to figure out if the basketball coach had anything to do with soft drinks, or maybe the athletic director. She'd be right there with me discussing these things. At the drop of a hat, she'd get a babysitter and go out to dinner with customers. She was always cheerful, happy, responsive and on our side. That's

awfully important when you're fighting all these battles."

One of those battles was keeping another of their businesses, Crisp Container, alive. Harry L. remembers the struggles when he started that business in 1996.

"It had some very tough years the first few years, it was losing money. I was trying to work it all out. A lot of people wanted me to sell it, including my son; he wanted to sell it, and I had the opportunity. Rosemary stepped forward and said, 'No, we're not going to sell that.' She said it was a good business, and we were going to make it succeed."

Of course, she was right. Crisp Container is doing very well.

"She was in our discussions all the time, advising. She had great instincts, great judgment, and she certainly made me a better person than I normally would have been, by her influence."

Like their dad, the Crisp children obviously were the beneficiaries of Rosemary's faith, hope and love.

Rosemary and Harry L. and their family at a New Year's Eve gathering. They are flanked by Cathy (left) and Cara; (standing) Carole, Bob and Cheryl Rabbitt, Cyndi and Keith Dickens, and Stacie and Harry 'Lee.'

The family gathers for a photo during a 2003 visit to Scarborough, Maine. Harry L. and Rosemary are surrounded by (clockwise from top left) Keith and Cyndi Dickens, Mark and Carole Schwarm, Cara and Chris Sims, Cheryl and Bob Rabbitt, Cathy Newbold, Harry 'Lee' and Stacie, who is holding Hallie.

Pride and Joy

This framed collection of the Crisp children as babies was displayed in their parents' bedroom on Suzanne Drive in Marion until the family moved into Crisp Acres, where Rosemary hung it in her dressing room. The children are (clockwise from top: Cathy, Cara, Cyndi, Harry 'Lee,' Carole and Cheryl.

'All that I am, or hope to be, I owe
to my angel mother. I remember her prayers,
and they have always followed me.
They have clung to me all my life.'

– Abraham Lincoln,
16th president of the United States

The family gathers for a portrait during a family trip to Blackberry Farm in Tennessee. They are (seated) Cheryl, Cathy and Carole; (standing) Bob Rabbitt, Stacie and Lee, Rosemary and Harry L., Chris and Cara, Cyndi and Keith, and Mark Schwarm.

*C*ara, the youngest of the six Crisp children, smiles as she recalls the look on her mom's face whenever she was around her family. "There was a twinkle in her eye."

And why wouldn't there be? Rosemary's greatest joy was her family.

"I chose to be a stay-at-home mother, and I wouldn't have had it any other way. Each of the kids is an individual. Erma Bombeck wrote in an article that which child you love the best is the one who needed you at the time. That always stuck with me, because that's true. At certain times, certain of your children require more of your attention. You love them all. There's a place in your heart for all of them. The kids had all gone together one time to buy me a mother's ring for Mother's Day. This had all of their birthstones in it. They're all in one ring, and there's a place for each stone in this ring, and that's exactly how my love is, and where there's a place in my heart for all of them. They are all in my heart."

As is she in theirs. Talk of her brings laughter at fond and enduring memories, along with tears that she is not with them in person to share in the heartfelt laughter. Though their reflections are tinged with that hint of sadness, it is the unconditional love and respect that stand out, along with the knowledge that while all moms are indeed special, Rosemary, in so many ways, was unique.

CYNDI CRISP DICKENS

The first child born to Rosemary and Harry L. bears more than a passing resemblance to her mom. And, like her mom, Cyndi had a passion for nursing. She earned a nursing degree, as well as a master's in business from Murray State University. That's also where she met husband Keith Dickens, who was a business major. Keith put himself through school working for Nabisco and calling on grocery stores.

"While we were dating, we would come home, and he and Dad would talk grocery business," Cyndi recalls.

In fact, the summer after his junior year, Keith signed on as a Pepsi MidAmerica employee; he worked for Harry L. for 14 years.

"We were really close for those 14 years with my mom and dad," Cyndi says.

Before she entered that stage in her life, Cyndi parlayed her nursing degree into a job at a pediatric hospital in Dallas. Though she and Keith moved back to this area after they married, Cyndi's nursing experience gave her insights that she felt could help her mom.

"My job was in patient education, and I knew from working with people with diabetes or heart conditions about patients taking care

Cyndi Crisp, a little ballerina.

First-born child Cyndi bears more than a passing resemblance to her mother, of whom she says 'Mom was a giver. She didn't say "What can be done for me?" If she was a part of a group, it was "How can I give back?"'

of themselves at home. I knew health support groups would be helpful. When Mom got ovarian cancer, I really wanted her to join a cancer support group, but she'd say, 'No, I'm really fine.' She didn't want to have to be taken care of."

So, when a cancer survivor at the Ocean Reef Club in Key Largo contacted her about joining a support group there, Rosemary declined, saying, "Really, I'm doing fine, I'm a nurse, so I kind of understand everything."

But, Cyndi says, the woman, obviously not easily deterred, realized how beneficial Rosemary's participation could be for others in the group.

"About the third time the lady contacted her, she said, 'Rosemary, you're a nurse, and you might be able to help someone out.' Mom thought about that and realized, 'Well, maybe I could.' So she went, and after the first time, she never quit going because she thought she could help others."

And that, quite simply, is how her mom lived her life.

"There are takers in life and there are givers," Cyndi says. "Mom was a giver. She didn't say, 'What can be done for me?' If she was part of a group, it was, 'How can I give back?' In the Bible, it says that much is expected to whom much is given. She never quoted that to me, but that was

Cyndi and her husband, Keith Dickens, with sons (from top) Harrison, Hunter and Hayden.

Mom. She was grateful for everything she had, but if she could give back, she did."

That's an attitude, a belief system, a way of living life, that Cyndi and all of her siblings inherited from their parents. Cyndi became more aware of just how much her parents gave back – in terms of philanthropy and community involvement – during and after college.

"We would tell them that there were things they were doing, things they were involved with, that should be in the newspaper, because bad things hit the papers sometimes.

But they'd say, 'No, that's OK,' and I'd say, 'People need to know you do good, too,' because we were protective of our parents. It hurt us when they were hurt. But, we really didn't dwell on those things as a family. We had fun together, we enjoyed each other's company. The few things that we felt were hurtful, we might discuss them, but then we moved on. If we were right with God, and we were right with each other, that was good and that was how you handled life."

Giving back in small ways is just as important as doing it on a large scale. Cyndi uses herself and her family as an example. The couple and their three children – Hunter, 18, Harrison, 16, and Hayden, 14 – live in Paducah, Ky., where the children attend Catholic school.

"Some parents come in, and they want to have their kids at the Catholic or Christian school, but if it doesn't meet their standards, they're out of there. We're not like that, we weren't raised like that. We want to know what we can do to make it better. If everybody leaves, nothing gets better. You dig in your heels, you roll up your sleeves, and you ask, 'What can we do?'"

That "stick-to-itiveness," as Cyndi calls it, is one of the many lessons she learned from her mom.

"And that's in everything, in your marriage, just loving what's good about people. It's about not judging or expecting too much, because you'll always be disappointed if you put expectations on people. But if you just love them and enjoy what they can give you, you'll be a lot happier,

and they'll feel that from you. You're going to be happier because they feel that love from you. That was a lot of the way Mom operated."

Cyndi has fond memories of her mom when she was healthy.

"People see pictures of her, and they remember her the last few years before she died. I think of her when she was healthy. My favorite pictures are when she was in her 40s, before all of the illness. I was born when she was 23; when I was 20, she was 43. She taught me how to be a mother with all of my siblings, feeding them, putting them to sleep. She taught me as a Girl Scout leader, as a nurse, as an executive's wife. I attended conventions for the soft drink business with Mom and Dad all over the world, and they taught me the value of listening. As a female, I identified with Mom."

It was because of Cyndi that Rosemary became a Girl Scout leader.

"I remember looking forward to becoming a Brownie, but I came home one day and was heartbroken, telling Mom that there was no Brownie leader. And here she is, with my dad's business growing, every two years she had a new baby, and she said, 'I'll be your Brownie leader.' She was my leader for 12 years in Girl Scouts. All my girlfriends loved my mom. She'd just give it her all, with projects, with campouts, she just took ownership to make things better.

"She tried really hard to do the best she could at what was before her. That then led her to something else. That was Mom."

Cyndi followed in her mother's footsteps and earned a degree in nursing and worked at Children's Medical Center in Dallas, Texas.

Rosemary with daughter Cathy during Christmas Eve with the family. 'I think of her daily,' Cathy says. 'She had such an impact on everyone's life.'

CATHY CRISP NEWBOLD

A scrap of paper holds great meaning for Rosemary and Harry L.'s second-oldest child. On it, someone had written, "The world is full of people who will go their whole lives and not live one day."

Her mom, Cathy says emphatically, "did not intend on being one of them. She lived every day to the fullest."

And Cathy certainly saw that first-hand. She left her job as a teacher's assistant for children with behavior disorders in the Marion school system, so she could devote her time to helping her mom.

"God truly blessed me with being able to take care of Mom for as long as I did," Cathy says, "and for this I'm truly grateful."

By the time Rosemary would call Cathy around 8 a.m. to let her know she was ready for the day, Rosemary's day was already three hours old. She wanted to be ready for appointments, meetings, phone calls and whatever else might be part of her always-hectic schedule, and that meant tending not only to normal morning routines, but to time-consuming daily medical treatments, including IVs, that Cathy sometimes helped with.

Rose Berkel (lower right) with her daughter, Rosemary; granddaughter Cathy Newbold and great-granddaughter Nicole Newbold.

Rosemary is surrounded by daughter Cathy; Cathy's daughter, Nicole; and Nicole's daughter, Elaine.

"I drove her around quite a bit, to doctor appointments, for treatments, to go shopping, to getting her hair done. She didn't like people to know she was sick. She didn't want people to feel sorry for her; she didn't want to be a burden to anyone. Mom wanted to enjoy life."

Rosemary's zest for life and the great joy she took in her children created memories of childhood that still evoke laughter. Holidays, of course, were special times. Cathy chuckles as she recalls a Halloween when she was very young, and Rosemary put quite a scare into her husband.

"Mom had gone into the attic and found one of my dad's old hunting jackets. She found a mask, put on the coat, and rang the front doorbell. She had forgotten to take her rings off, so she kept her hands in her pockets. Dad got to the door, and she just refused to talk. He had these little kids around and didn't know what to think; finally she pulled off the mask, and he was floored. She had a great sense of humor."

Decorating the Christmas tree together was always an important tradition, even after the children were grown and out of the house. When they were youngsters, Rosemary always made sure, especially for holidays, that they were properly attired.

"She dressed all of us alike; the girls were in the same exact clothes," Cathy recalls. "I don't know how she did it, but she did. Our hair was done the same way. I admire how she took the time to do that plus get herself ready."

Even Girl Scout campouts at Little Grassy Lake, near Marion, were special family events. Rosemary, as the troop leader, always stayed in the cabin or tents with the Girl Scouts. Harry L. would stay in the camper with some of Cathy's younger siblings. Whatever the activity – pitching tents, cooking on the open fire, eating "s'mores" – Rosemary always made sure her troop members were learning and having fun. She even made hiking memorable.

"We'd go hiking, but not just on any trail," Cathy says. "Mom would have someone go out before all the rest of us to rub onion on the trees. You had to smell the trees to figure out which way to go."

Second-born daughter, Cathy.

Cathy Newbold's family: (Clockwise from left)
Children Tyler, Cameron and Nicole,
and granddaughter Elaine.

One camping trip, on a particularly cold and snowy night, brings back warm memories.

"A cozy fire kept us warm inside the cabin," Cathy recalls. "All the girls were scattered on the floor in their sleeping bags, and I was still awake watching the fire die down. Out of the corner of my eye, I see a shadowy figure carefully, quietly walking through all the girls in their sleeping bags. The fire had died down, and the cabin was getting colder. But there was enough of a glow to light up Mom's face. She was all dressed and bringing firewood in early in the morning so we would be warm. She stoked the fire and added more wood. She could have assigned this to any of the girls, but she did it herself. I was amazed when she got up early the next morning to go hiking after being up most of the night taking care of everyone else. She always amazed me with how she was always thinking of others."

Rosemary made every day special for Cathy and her siblings.

"When we were little, she always greeted us at the door after school. She was always there for us. And we always saw Mom and Dad showing how much they loved each other. They were always holding hands, touching each other, saying 'I love you' to each other, complimenting each other. They were truly soul mates."

For Cathy, a mother of three – Nicole, who is 30; Tyler, who is 28; and Cameron, who is 26 – and grandmother of Nicole's 6-year-old daughter, Elaine, the importance of keeping family close is but one of many of life's lessons she learned from Rosemary.

"I learned to put God and prayer first in your life. I learned patience, kindness, to treat people with respect, to never let an opportunity pass to help someone, to leave things better than when you found them, to never let the sun go down on an argument, to embrace the good times as well as the bad, because bad times make you stronger. Mom was a wonderful teacher."

Like her siblings, Cathy frequently saw how much Rosemary loved being among people.

"She loved to people watch. We would be somewhere, standing in a line or even just walking by someone. She would stop them and say, 'I really like your blouse.' She always taught me to never pass up an opportunity to pay someone a compliment. 'It will probably make their day,' she would tell me. 'People love compliments, people love to smile.' She'd go out of her way to brighten people's day. Why not? That's just who she was."

Her mom was a woman of faith, of great strength, of character.

"I think of her daily. It's still hard for me to talk about her. She had such an impact on everyone's life."

'My mom was amazing,' says Cheryl. 'Her sacrifices are forever etched in our minds now that we are mothers.'

CHERYL CRISP RABBITT

Cheryl, the third child born to Rosemary and Harry L., loves to share a special story about her mom, one that makes her laugh but that she also tells with a tone of voice that, even to this day, suggests just a bit of disbelief. But, it is a true story of a pope and a picture.

During a trip to Rome in 1992, Rosemary and Harry L., her brother Jim, and his wife, Sue, had an opportunity to meet Pope John Paul II. And Rosemary couldn't help but show the Holy Father a picture of her children.

"She's there meeting the most influential Christian man in the world," Cheryl says, somewhat incredulously, "And what is she doing? She's asking him to 'Please pray for our family,' and saying, 'These are my children, and I'm so proud of them.' I wouldn't even have bothered him with that. But, you know what? It was so important to her that she wanted him to pray for her children. That's just how sweet she was."

Cheryl believes a very different kind of meeting, one that she witnessed, also speaks volumes about her mom. This

Cheryl's first Holy Communion.

occurred at the 2001 inauguration of President George W. Bush, which Rosemary and Harry L. attended with Cheryl and her family.

"She had been going through cancer treatment, and she was very thin, so she was wearing a mink coat. She wasn't wearing it to be pretentious, she was wearing it for warmth. There were some protesters there and one of them insulted her about wearing a mink coat. She looked at him and said, 'If you were a gentleman, you wouldn't talk to a lady like that.' I wanted to strangle the guy; he was yelling in her face. He was so rude to her. I was offended; I wanted to protect her. What she said to him was so sweet and kind — it just changed the situation. It humbled him because she wasn't mean back to him. Now that I'm raising teenagers, I understand why my mom said that. It's amazing how, as I get older, little bits of her wisdom come to me."

The anecdotes about the pope and the protester illustrate, as Cheryl calls it, the "essence" of her mom.

"My mom was the same person out in public as she was at home. Many people are good, but there are very few people in this world who I think are pure. She had so much sweet innocence. She didn't think badly of people.

"My mom and dad were very blessed to experience life to the fullest – to be able to meet many wonderful people and to travel to incredible destinations. Mom never, ever thought she was above anyone. Each person was equally important to her. She treated each person the same regardless of their social status … the waiter or bus boy at the table, the janitor, the person holding the elevator door. She was always so kind and sweet and pure. It was amazing how she really valued everyone."

A warm smile crosses Cheryl's face as she describes her mom as "Audrey Hepburn, Jackie Kennedy and Princess Diana all rolled into one. She was full of class. There was a femininity, a purity, a sweetness about her."

Rosemary's key lessons to her children, of course, were that faith and family must be central in their lives.

"You have to make it a top priority, you have to work at it," Cheryl says. "We are so thankful for everything, and we always say how blessed we are. Even when Mom was sick, I cannot remember her ever complaining.

"Never," she stresses. "There are some days I say to myself, 'I'm just not as strong as my mother,' here I have four kids,

she had six; she got sick; she lost babies; she had cancer. Then I remember her saying, 'If you're having a bad day, go have your pity party for a few moments, cry, get it out, and then get on with your day.' It's true. It's OK to cry and release that stress and then feel better about it."

Rosemary always was setting an example for the children simply by being herself. They are, of course, lessons well remembered.

"My mom was amazing. Her sacrifices are forever etched in our minds now that we are mothers," Cheryl says. "Even if we were camping out in the middle of nowhere, on Sunday we had to drive until we would find a church. If we missed Mass – and we rarely missed Mass – we'd have our own, all of us."

At St. Joseph's in Marion, "She'd line us up, matching dresses, matching hair bows, and sit us in the front row. If we misbehaved, we got the pinch. We knew we were expected to behave. And if not, there was a consequence. She was firm but gentle. She expected you to be respectful and she would respect you."

Her choice to be a stay-at-home mom meant driving the kids to school, being home at the end of their day, being a Girl Scout leader – it meant being very involved in their lives. But another of Rosemary's lessons stemmed from her commitment to maintaining a strong marriage with Harry L.

"She would always travel with my father – not a lot – they took one big trip a year," Cheryl says. "Mom said, 'I'm not going to be the type of wife who stays home while her husband travels. I can see where businessmen would travel with their secretaries, but I'm going to be there with my husband.' She always said, 'The best gift I can give you is I can love your father. When you grow up and move away and have your own families, I need to be here for your father.' She let us know that we were totally loved, but it was important for her and Dad to have a relationship also. So, one time a year, she and Dad would go on a trip. But Mom was there for all of our activities when we were younger. She was very involved in whatever we were doing but she also was helping with Dad's business."

Rosemary mentored in less obvious ways as well.

"She always had a Bible by her bed," Cheryl says. "I started to lay something on it, and she'd always be so gentle,

Cheryl and her family (clockwise from center back) Ryan, husband Bob, Olivia, Alexandra and Taylor.

Rosemary with Cheryl's children (from left) Alexandra, Taylor, Ryan and Olivia. The photo was taken in November 2007, the day Rosemary went into the hospital for the last time.

but she said, 'Don't do that.' To her it wasn't respectful, even to put a vase of flowers on it. She was just so gentle."

About a month before Rosemary passed, Harry L. alerted Cheryl that her mom wasn't doing well.

"Dad would tell me what was going on, that she wasn't feeling well. But she didn't want us to worry. Even at the end, she wouldn't complain."

Cheryl needed to be at her mom's side, knowing also that that meant leaving husband Bob at their home in Annapolis, Md., to juggle work and the many responsibilities that come with four children – Ryan, now 19, Olivia, 17, Taylor, 15, and Alexandra, 13.

"My husband was so understanding," she says, pausing as emotion washes over her. "It was wonderful being with Mom that last month. He stayed with the kids, he took them to school. He even flew out, and at one point I told him I was going to come home, and he told me I needed to stay here. I have always been so thankful for that."

When Cheryl decided that she needed to come to Marion, she also decided to make it a surprise. She laughs as she remembers being the one who was surprised.

"I came to the house, and I expected to see her in bed, not feeling well, no makeup on, and I walk in and say,

'I'm here.' And Mom and Dad weren't even there. They were out to lunch, so I went to the restaurant. Mom later told me that she said to Dad at the restaurant, 'That girl right there, she looks so much like Cheryl.' She was so excited to see me. She just wasn't going to let the cancer stop her from living every day."

To Cheryl, her mom radiated elegance.

"Mom was elegant, not so much how she looked but how she carried herself. That's one thing that I hope my daughters can learn from her, that she was such a beautiful person inside. A lot of people are attractive on the outside, and Mom was incredibly beautiful. But her beauty was also on the inside, even though she was attractive on the outside, her inner beauty was always shining through."

Rosemary touched not only her family, but so many others, with her gentle, kind, sweet nature, and her strength of character.

"I think that came from her Bible, and her Rosary. She would say her Rosary every night. I like to think of her in bed, looking up to heaven and talking to her 'Father' in heaven before she went to sleep. It brought her such strength, courage and peace."

Cheryl reacts to being crowned Miss Illinois National Teen-ager 1982.

CAROLE CRISP SCHWARM

Carole, Rosemary and Harry L.'s fourth child has so many favorite memories of her mom that it's difficult to choose only one.

"My mom could bring happiness, joy and fun to anything. One year for Halloween, she turned the basement laundry room and bathroom of our childhood home into a haunted house, with a bowl of olives as eyeballs, spaghetti as the brain and stewed tomatoes as the heart. On April Fool's Day, she made green eggs and ham. On Valentine's Day, you awoke to a box of sweets on your plate at breakfast. She loved the Christmas season, and our home was always decorated from top to bottom with garland, trees, Christmas music, nativity scenes and cinnamon candles burning. She would have a fire burning in the fireplace almost year 'round, regardless of the season. We grew up in a very happy home. With so many children, I don't know how she accomplished so much. Her demeanor always stayed the same; she always made things better. As I became older, she was not only my mother, but she became my friend.

"My mother was a passionate woman. She had a passion for life, a passion to live and lived fully until God called her home. Love and kindness overflowed from her. When I remember my mother, I often think of Proverbs 31:25-31, 'She is a woman of strength and dignity, and has no fear of old age. When she speaks, her words are wise, and kindness is the rule for everything she says. She watches carefully all that goes on throughout her household, and is never lazy. Her children stand and bless her; so does her husband. He praises her with these words, "There are many fine women in the world, but you are the best of them all." Charm can be deceptive, and beauty doesn't last, but a woman who fears and reverences God shall greatly be praised. Praise her for the many fine things she does. These good deeds of hers shall bring her honor and recognition from people of importance.'

"There was an essence of joy, kindness, patience and faithfulness that radiated from my mother. You often hear this about people who have a deep faith in God. Even with her suffering so much, you still saw her essence; it was still completely her."

Of course, at the heart of that essence was Rosemary's faith.

"I don't mean her faith as far as being consistent and loyal about going to Mass, which she was. She rarely missed Mass, even if she wasn't feeling well. But it was her true belief, and the depth of it, in God, and her dependency on Him. It was so deep internally in her, it was never questioned. Often, when people would describe my mom, they would say that there was just something different about her, a light that came from her, and a joy that always came from her. I believe that stems from her true humble belief and trust in God. She was a very humble woman."

Carole, like all of her siblings, shares that deep faith. In fact, when she was dating her future husband, Mark, she asked him to never ask her to change her Catholic faith. When Carole married Mark in 2002, she instantly had a family that included Mark's two sons, Jacob, now 21, and Jeremiah, now 19. That was a first for the Crisp family.

"We had never had stepchildren in our family. I wasn't sure how to handle the transition into becoming a mother of two small boys. Immediately, my mom counted them as her grandchildren, and loved them as such. She was a tremendous support for Mark and me. When you blend a family, you're not always quite sure how to handle different situations: Are these my children? Are these my stepchildren? I have been unable to have children, which is funny in my family. It's a cross I've been asked to bear, so I try to unite my cross with the Lord's cross. I am blessed and

Rosemary painted this picture for Carole, her fourth child.

Carole, here with Harry L. and Rosemary, says she learned from her mother that regardless of what life presents, accept it with grace and compassion. 'My mom showed us how to do everything with dignity,' Carole says.

thankful to have Jacob and Jeremiah as my sons and in my life. They have been a true joy, and they have taught me many great things."

Carole learned from her mom that regardless of what life presents, accept it with grace and compassion. "My mom showed us by her example how to do everything with dignity. She didn't try to do that; it was just who she was as a human being."

Everything, of course, including cancer, which Carole says her mom handled "elegantly."

"To her, this was something that God had allowed her to go through, and she was going to do her best with this task that God had asked her to carry. She prayed that she would be healed, but only if it was His will and what He thought it should be. But if she wouldn't be healed, then she asked that it be allowed to touch people and grow her as a person."

When Rosemary accepted her Inspiring Woman award at Southern Illinois University Carbondale in October 2007, even though Carole and other family members obviously knew how ill she was, the experience proved to be somewhat of a revelation.

"When my mom finally passed, a person could see it as, 'She finally gets to rest from this battle she has waged for such a long time.' We didn't see it that way. She always got well. She was always well again. She handled her illness so beautifully that we didn't see our mom as being sick. We knew she had this illness to deal with. But I think when she went up to receive the Inspiring Woman's Award, and I sat back and saw her from afar – seeing that she needed assistance - that's when I realized that this time it was different. That was one of my harder times – realizing that the illness was really taking over. And it was almost astonishing. It's not that it was ignored in any way; it's that she didn't live her life like an ill person. She got up every morning, and she got dressed; there was a whole world out there for her to see and accomplish things in. Nothing was going to stop my

Horses were a big part of Crisp family life, as seen in this photo of Rosemary and Carole. Rosemary had purchased a new saddle for Harry L., for his birthday, and she decided to try it out.

mom from making the most of every day. Nothing.

"Taking care of her often meant trying to keep up with her. Sometimes I told her, 'Mom, I know you still want to run errands, but I've got to go home, I'm tired, I can't do it anymore,'" Carole says, laughing. "She was that kind of person. We didn't see her sitting around in a bathrobe feeling sorry for herself. Ever."

Hard as it was to watch her cope with her illness, Carole says it was her mom who did the comforting. "She constantly comforted us. It is much easier to care for someone who loves God, who's not afraid, who is not a complainer, who is happy and joyful. When my mom was in the hospital dying, she continued to comfort us. That was amazing to me. No matter how much we tried to comfort her, she was still loving and holding us."

Carole doesn't hesitate to give her dad credit for the adjustments he had to make as her mom's health deteriorated. "They were so close. I had to watch my dad make such changes, even in caring for my mother. He is a determined and successful businessman (with a great sense of humor, I might add!); that was his role in the family, and he went out and earned a living. Mom was a stay-at-home mom, and she took care of the children. For her to need extra care, I couldn't have asked for anything more from my dad; he was there for her every step of the way. He loved her unconditionally and never looked at her any differently – even when she had lost all of her hair. He was crazy about her."

Not long after Rosemary passed, a conversation with her dad helped Carole recognize that the dynamics of her relationship with him had also changed. "I underestimated all the losses that you have with one loss," Carole says. "You go through not only just losing your mother, but all the parts of her personality, all the dependency you had on her. I underestimated how much she helped with my relationship with my dad. If I needed to talk about something, if I was unsure how to handle a situation with my father, I

Carole studied
tap-dancing.

would bring it to her, and she would help me soften it, and then I could go to him. So then I had to mourn that loss, realizing that I didn't have that anymore. I had to alter and mature in myself a new relationship with my father, one that was not through my mother. I now enjoy a new relationship and friendship with my father."

Carole is proud of her parents' commitment to each other and the example they set.

"She was everything. She did everything. All the business dinner meetings he went to, she went with him. My mom and dad never took separate vacations. She was his business confidante, his best friend, the mother of his children and his traveling companion. There's a lot to be said for that. They were married almost 50 years, with six children, in what continues to be a very close-knit family. In these days and times, that is almost looked upon as unnecessary. But in a time when the divorce rate is high and families are divided, it is amazing – and continues to be a blessing – to see two people who were so wholeheartedly committed to each other. There could not be a higher reward

bestowed on our mother than the way her children look at her, even now after she has been gone, with all of the love and respect in the world. She could have been anything – a Mother Teresa, even – and we couldn't have respected her more. We value her, and we know how much she gave and sacrificed. Sacrifice seems to be something we don't want in our society. She sacrificed for her children, her husband and her God, and because of that she became an incredible woman."

Mark and Carole on their wedding day with Mark's sons, Jacob (left) and Jerimiah. Carole says her mother immediately counted the boys as her grandchildren.

The Schwarm family: Jacob, Carole, Mark and Jerimiah.

HARRY LEE CRISP III

The second-youngest of the six Crisp children is, by his own admission, "very Type A, very business-oriented." It appears that's been the case for Lee, the president and chief operating officer of Pepsi MidAmerica, since a very young age.

"When I was a young child, I got in deep trouble with my mom. Mom and Dad would get all of these magazines, and I thought, 'That's an opportunity.' I must have been 8. I went door to door down our street, with year-old magazines, and I sold them for whatever I could get."

He laughs as he remembers what came next.

"I got home, and my mom was in such disbelief. She asked, 'What did you do?' She took me into my father and he said, 'What did Lee do?' She told him, and he was so proud. She made me go back and give back all that money. Later, she laughed about it. And I can see it with my kids, you can see little hints of what they may become. No one prompted me to do that, I just did it naturally."

That was the case by the time he reached seventh-grade, also.

"One day, I got up, I put on a tie and took a briefcase to school. I did that for months. No one told me to; I just wanted to be a businessman so bad."

But before that could happen, there was plenty of growing up to do. In the summer before eighth grade, Lee followed in his dad's footsteps and went to the Culver Academies, college preparatory boarding schools for boys and girls in Culver, Ind., for summer camp. That began a 13-year stretch of Lee being away from home, spending his high school years at Culver Military Academy, earning bachelor's degrees in music performance and business from Southern Illinois University in Carbondale, and spending four years in the Marine Corps.

Today, Lee and his family live in the home in Marion he grew up in. Lee and Stacie, who dated for seven years, married in 2000. They have two children, Laura Hallie, who is 8, and Harry Lee Crisp IV, who is 6, who they call Harry. While devoted to his profession, Lee is also a devoted family man, and he knows his mom was proud of the son who became a dad.

Harry 'Lee' Crisp with wife Stacie, Harry Lee IV and Hallie.

"She taught us, and showed us, the importance of love of family and extended family, of expressing your love and appreciation toward others while they can enjoy it," he says. "I'm very active with my kids. Every Saturday is my daughter's special day. We get up early, we go to the store, and she gets a star donut with sprinkles on it. I get my coffee, we sit down and we talk. Every Sunday morning is my son's special day. We go to a restaurant, and we have breakfast together. I try to have a balance."

Harry 'Lee,' here in the 5th grade.

And while it may not be apparent to many, the hard-charging businessman and former Marine inherited his mom's artistic ability. Rosemary was shocked by that realization, Lee recalls, laughing.

"When she heard I was re-doing my house, she thought, 'Oh my gosh, a Marine re-doing his house. Black, brown, camouflage colors, stainless steel.' And when she came

Harry 'Lee' Crisp III poses with his parents, Rosemary and Harry L., on Lee's wedding day, April 8, 2000.

Harry L. and Rosemary with Stacie and Harry 'Lee' Crisp in Clark, Colo., on a family trip.

over, she was shocked. Funny thing is, she started taking her friends over to see my house; that's how pleased she was. And then when she started re-doing her stables and the motor coach building, she copied my floors, my wall colors, my choices. That kind of opened her eyes a little bit."

There was much that Lee respected about his mom, including what he calls "the beauty of simplicity." He uses a story about Michelangelo to illustrate his point.

"He wanted to prove he was the greatest artist in the world. They asked him to prove it, and what he ended up doing to prove it, he drew a circle freehand and it was perfect. My mom was that way. What you get out of her simplicity was her beauty. Those little phrases of hers. They're so simple, but when you think about it, they're so deep and true. She would say, 'Why worry when you

can pray?' I'll say that to my wife now, because it's true. 'Is God in charge, or is He not in charge?' There's only one answer to that question in my mind. My mom always said, 'Why worry when you can just pray?' If you pray about it, He's looking after your best interests. It was her simplicity. Have faith. Raise your kids a certain way. All that simplicity turned out to be very beautiful."

Faith was never more important than throughout his mom's illness.

"Why do bad things happen to good people?" he asks, rhetorically. "God allows, but does not cause, certain things to happen to create a greater good. In Mom's physical weakness, she personified faithfulness and obedience to God."

Even during those trials, "She showed us selflessness, devotion and concern for others."

Harry 'Lee' says that even during his mother's hardest challenges, 'In Mom's physical weakness, she personified faithfulness and obedience to God. ... She showed us selflessness, devotion and concern for others.'

CARA CRISP SIMS

The youngest of Rosemary and Harry L.'s children laughs heartily when she thinks about what childhood was like with five siblings.

"Crazy good. Crazy."

Surrounded by mayhem, it's no surprise that Rosemary would want to have, as Cara calls it, "her time" each day.

"She would send us down to the basement and shut the door. She was so smart; boy, I wish I had a basement," she says of her Paducah home, thinking about her and husband Chris' three youngsters, Palmer, 7; Luke, 5; and Audrey Rosemary, 3. "All of us kids would go play, so she could cook dinner. She'd tell us to go play 'and unless you're bleeding or really hurt, do not open that door.'"

Her memories of that time are fond, reflections of growing up in a "good, old-fashioned" home.

"We weren't allowed to watch TV during the week. We played. We went camping a lot. Without making it sound too much like it was 'Leave it to Beaver,' it was that way. We had dinner together. Mom was head of Brownies. Mom took us, mainly by herself, to church. All those kids, how tired she must have been, but that was important to her. Even if we were out of town, you don't ever miss church."

Along with so many other traits, Rosemary passed along to her children her love of holidays.

"Every holiday was important to Mom," Cara says, smiling. "And she passed that down to me. Every Valentine's Day, I get the heart placemats out. For the Fourth of July, it could be stickers on the windows. Whatever the holiday, you've got decorations throughout the house."

Cara Crisp as a youngster.

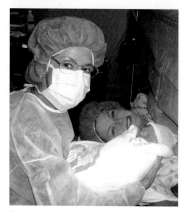

Rosemary was present at the birth of every grandchild, with the exception of Audrey Rosemary. Here she is with Cara and newborn Luke.

As a teenager, Cara learned lessons from her mom about not being judgmental. Of course, because she was a teen, the lessons weren't obvious. As an adult, Cara looks back with gratitude at the example Rosemary set.

"She was so unique, especially with five girls, just her characteristics. This may seem silly, but for example, women gossiping. Mom never did that. You know most women gossip; they'll see someone and say, 'Look what she has on.' And with five girls, you know how some people can get so involved with their daughters' lives, who they hang out with, things like that. My mom did none of that. She just had an innocence about her.

"When I was in high school, I was with my mom and pointed out someone and said to her, 'See that girl over there? She's not very nice to me. I don't like her.' As soon as I passed by her, my mom just stopped, smiled and said 'Hi' to her. I asked, being immature of course, 'Why did you do that?' It was because she saw nothing but good in people."

What Cara came to realize, she says, is that her mom "was happy all the time, she was just sweet. I've never met anyone like her, with her sweetness, her kindness, how her mind was built, her faith in God. Special is a very good word for her."

Special is also how Rosemary made the children feel — each of them.

"Out of six kids, I can honestly say there was never, ever a favorite. Never would she talk bad about a sibling in front of another one. Whoever needed her the most, whatever they were going through in their life, she

Luke, Cara, Audrey Rosemary, Chris and Palmer on the beach during a family vacation. Cara says of her mother, 'I've never met anyone like her, with her sweetness, her kindness, how her mind was built, her faith in God. Special is a very good word for her.'

would stop everything and make that her focus. You did feel special because you knew she would be there, no matter how busy she was, even with all those kids, even with all of her commitments. It didn't matter if it was something big in your life that was a negative, or something positive. She'd always find a way to be there."

After earning her teaching degree at the University of Tennessee-Martin, Cara moved to Nashville, where she taught for five years. Rosemary found a way to be there, driving with Cara to Nashville to help her get settled, and, of course, helping with the decorating of that first apartment.

And when grandchildren came along, Rosemary not only was on hand for each birth, she was on hand to help during those first challenging days at home.

"She loved newborns. Whenever we'd have our kids, she'd come and stay with us a couple of nights. I had Palmer, my oldest, and he wouldn't sleep, and I was inexperienced. He'd cry and cry. Mom took him that first night, so Chris and I could sleep. We slept for 4 1/2 hours, and when we woke up, there she was in the chair, asleep, holding the baby."

Cara always found her mom inspiring, perhaps even more so during Rosemary's years with cancer.

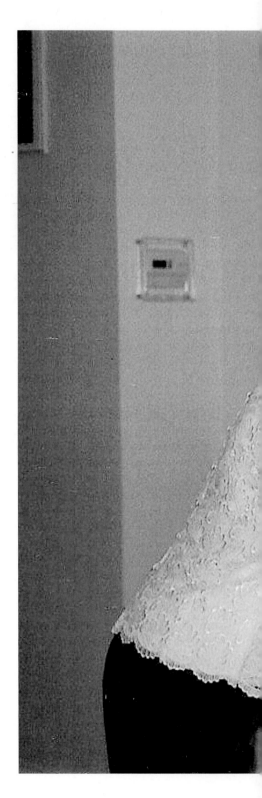

"Her famous response was, 'Why not me?' I sometimes feel like the reason she had cancer was that we got to see her star shine for 12 years. That was the one gift that her cancer gave everyone, to see how tough she was and humble, and that is something that her illness revealed. If she was never going to get cancer, we'd always know how sweet she was, but there was so much more. My gosh, from the colostomy bag, to continuing to travel, to not feeling well and literally having a fever from chemo and still going to dinners and doing everything that she did. You never saw her lying on a couch. None of us can hold a candle to her. Every time I have the flu or a headache, I feel so guilty complaining. She'd cry, she'd have her pity party, and say, 'OK, I've had my five-minute pity party, it's time to move on.' She was so inspiring."

What Cara learned from her mom, she says without hesitation, is, "Everything. Everything good."

"It didn't matter who you were or what you did, she was kind to everyone," Cara adds. "Each nurse who came in to her hospital room, and this was three or four days before she died, every time, Mom would ask, 'How are you doing today?' or 'What do you have going on this weekend?' She was just always wanting to know about each person. She was so full of kindness, her heart was just big and pure. And that's important to me, because I don't think a lot of people know that about her. Mom had pure thoughts in everything. I think that's just how you're built. She had a purity to her, from her marriage to Dad, to how she raised us kids, to how she looked at people, to her opinions about things, about how she reacted to cancer.

There was just a soft purity about her with everything in her life."

Special moments between Rosemary and Cara include a visit at Mayo Clinic (above) and during Cara's wedding rehearsal dinner.

Unshakable Faith

Pope John Paul II blesses a rosary for Rosemary during a trip to Rome in 1992. The rosary was inscribed with the words 'Faith, Hope, Love.'

'Every tomorrow has two handles.
We can seize it with the handle of anxiety,
or the handle of faith.'

— Henry Ward Beecher (1813-1887), American clergyman

aith was Rosemary's compass. Her own version of Henry Ward Beecher's observation, oft-repeated throughout her life, was, "Why worry when you can pray?"

Her faith was not based on circumstance or convenience. It simply was part of her being. Even as cancer took its toll, Rosemary remained serene. Daughter Cheryl recalls one of her mom's last days at home in late 2007.

"It was well before 6 a.m., and she had taken a shower and was getting ready for her day. I was sitting in the bathroom with her because she was thin, shaky and had lost a lot of weight. I didn't want her to lose her balance. Usually, one of us daughters was in the bathroom as she got ready. We would cry, laugh, hug Mom and just enjoy these special moments with her.

"On this morning, as I watched her, and all of the daily medical care she had to go through, I thought of how a normal person would complain or give up. Her 'normal' daily routine of IVs and medicine would exhaust anyone. I looked at her face, and she did what she had to do with love, patience and an actual sense of calm and purpose. I was struck by the beautiful expression on her face, almost like an angel. I wondered what made her so strong and determined. I looked at her and said, 'Mom, how can you be so joyful when there are so many grumpy people in the world?'

"Mom stopped what she was doing. She looked me straight in the face and smiled, 'Because, Honey, I am going to see the face of Jesus soon.' Our mother knew she was going to die and go to heaven. She was just waiting for God to open the door, call her name and welcome her home."

As her priest at St. Joseph parish in Marion and close family friend, Father Richard Mohr, says, "One thing that was obvious was her faith. If you knew Rosemary, you knew what she believed. She let everyone know that, she was extremely comfortable. Her Catholic faith was the most important thing. That characteristic of her, that faith, it was just a

Rosemary Berkel (lower right) at her first Holy Communion. With her are (left to right) Marjorie Dalmer, her mother Rose Berkel and Mrs. Harpstrite.

Father Richard Mohr blesses the Crisps' boat.

defining thing. And it was solid. Some people, when they are sick, they don't want others to know. She wanted people to know. She said, 'After all, I want them to pray for me.' One of her good lines was, 'Look at what has happened here since I've been sick. I've got people praying who hadn't prayed for years.'"

Father Rich, now retired, first encountered Rosemary when he came to St. Joseph's in July 1990.

"I think I met her the first morning; she came to Mass. She used to come to daily Mass a lot. And from that point on, we were friends. I'm serious; it was that immediate. Rosemary was unbelievable in that sense. My opening remarks at her funeral were quoting Edna St. Vincent Millay's poem, 'The presence of that absence is everywhere.'

"It only grew from there. We simply clicked. She had a way of reaching out. Her faith was so integral in her life. There was nothing phony there. One of the main things in our faith is reaching out, helping others. She was a nurse, and if there was anything anyone needed, she was there. She believed very strongly in volunteering."

As is true today with her own family, Rosemary's deep faith can be traced to growing up in a devoutly Catholic home.

"It was imbedded in us that we always prayed before meals and always said our night prayers," she recalled. "During Lent, we'd always go on Wednesday and Friday in the evening to special services. Your life revolved around your church a lot."

That devotion included Saturday catechism classes, where Rosemary studied the Catholic faith, learning and memorizing many stories and prayers. She enjoyed these studies, as well as the friendships she developed with her classmates. Though her girlfriends may have been out playing in the neighborhood, Rosemary never was one to try to get out of the classes.

Her faith sustained her throughout her life. Rosemary found it growing even stronger after receiving her ovarian cancer diagnosis early in 1996.

"Having faith in God means I'm never alone," she said in 2000. "When I've had to go to surgery and a family member couldn't be there, or when family members had to be gone, I never, never feel I'm alone. I feel like God's

out there. I pray to Jesus, and I ask Mary and Joseph to pray for me, too. It's just so reassuring to me, and it took me a long time in life to learn to do this. I think really until I had my first bout with cancer; actually, about five years ago now, when I really started thinking more deeply. I always had this faith, and I used to say I hope I get to heaven. I don't say that anymore. I say, 'When I get to heaven.' Everything that's happened in my life has been up to Him, my joys, my sufferings, and I've had a few sufferings. And I plan someday that Jesus, Mary and Joseph will come and get me and take me to heaven when I die."

"I Can Only Imagine" was one of the songs played over and over in Rosemary's hospital room during her last few days.

Her mom, daughter Carole says, "didn't just have her faith, she had a relationship with God."

"People can have a faith and say, 'I believe, I believe,' but hers was a personal relationship. She talked to God every day. It wasn't just a faith where she read the Bible, which she did, and went to Mass. It went deeper than that. She had that deep relationship with God. She talked with Him, she trusted Him, she asked Him questions, she would ask for guidance. She really utilized that relationship."

Rosemary led the entire family on a religious retreat to Medjugorje, Bosnia-Herzegovina, in 1988 to visit the shrine of Our Lady of Medugorje. In 1981, six young people reported seeing an apparition of the Virgin Mary, and the small village became a destination for pilgrims. Over the years, visitors have reported a variety of phenomena, including seeing the sun spin or being surrounded by such objects as crosses and hearts.

"While we were there, Mom saw the miracle of the sun spinning and later her Rosary turned from silver to gold," notes daughter Cheryl, adding that Rosemary made pilgrimages to the village on two other occasions.

In son Lee's eyes, his mom was given the gift of faith.

"Everyone has a gift. She's the closest one I've ever seen to have that gift, a child-like faith. It seems from Day 1 she felt, 'God and my relationship are this way,' and she was unwavering. If you stepped back and watched her over time, it's real, it's true; and you can watch God around her, you could see it around her, with people. It was amazing how she enjoyed people, whether a janitor or the chairmen of companies, she had a glow about her when she talked with them."

Dr. Brigitte A. Barrette, who not only treated Rosemary during the 12 years she lived with ovarian cancer, but became very close friends with her, echoes that sentiment.

"I have rarely seen someone with so much faith. I have not had many patients telling me that, as she used to say, her disease was the gift of God. It may have made it more acceptable to her, but that is how she was dealing with it. I think of her raising all the children in the Catholic faith. Despite the fact that Harry wasn't a Catholic at the time, she made it a point to bring them to church every week. It was a very strong commitment, it was a beautiful gift that she had. Faith is a gift; she had that gift."

To her husband of nearly 48 years, there is no question that God was the major influence in Rosemary's life.

"I'm not an overly religious person, but certainly I saw where there was God's influence in this whole thing, because I just saw too much; there was more to this than meets the eye," Harry L. says. "Rosemary would lose something, she said a prayer to St. Anthony, the patron saint of lost things, and she'd find it. That was her whole life. I never saw it fail, and I'm talking about a woman I was married to for nearly 48 years. We'd have an event outside, a wedding, a social event or a political event, and she would pray for good weather, and the clouds would just seem to part. After a while, even a hard-nosed businessman has to say, 'There's more to this than I'm aware of.'"

To Father Rich, Rosemary "so exemplified what our faith really means; you saw how she reached out." At Rosemary's funeral, he offered a special eulogy, describing his good friend as an apostle to the apostles.

"I referred to Mary Magdalene and the gospel. She is the first one our Lord appears to, and she is to announce to the apostles that He has risen. She was the apostle to the apostles; apostle means to be sent, she was sent. Rosemary was like an apostle.

"She shared her faith with everyone."

Father Richard Mohr, delivering a message to the congregation, says Rosemary 'so exemplified what our faith really means; you saw how she reached out ... She shared her faith with everyone.'

Pope John Paul II offers
a blessing for the Crisp children
during the trip to Rome in 1992.

Women's Health Conference

Rosemary signs a document proclaiming the Women's Health Conference. With her are (left to right) Cathy Wood, Fran Becque and Ann Knewitz. The women, led by Rosemary, created the conference, which celebrated 25 years in September 2011.

'One of the deep secrets of life is
that all that is really worth the doing
is what we do for others.'

— Lewis Carroll, English writer

Neither woman could have known it at the time, but the seeds for the Women's Health Conference that Rosemary and Ann Knewitz co-founded in 1986, in fact, were sown some 30 years earlier.

While Rosemary pursued her nursing degree between 1955 and 1958 at St. Mary's Hospital School of Nursing in Evansville, Ind., Ann was working as a dietitian at Marion Memorial Hospital. Ann first noticed Rosemary while she was volunteering there.

"Rosemary was still a student nurse in Evansville, and she was at the hospital, talking with everyone," Ann recalls. "I didn't know her, I didn't go up and talk to her, but I'm looking at this person, very attractive, very personable, and I had this instant admiration."

After graduation, Rosemary returned to Marion Memorial to fulfill her scholarship obligation, pursuing the profession she adored. Though they worked in the same building, their paths didn't cross very often. Nonetheless, Ann says, "Rosemary was just a figure you would know. She definitely had a presence. One time, I was a patient, and she sent me flowers. And I didn't know her that well."

In those days, the hospital didn't have a waiting room. People who came in for lab work or X-rays sat in a hallway while waiting their turn.

"Rosemary would come in for work through the back door, and she would have to pass by all these people," Ann said. "Our administrative assistant's office was in that area, and he would stand at his open door and watch her come in and speak to everyone along the way. One day he said to me, 'She's nice to everybody.' I could almost cry when I think about that."

While Rosemary chose to become a stay-at-home mom, Ann continued working at the hospital. If a member of the Crisp family needed some medical advice, perhaps for allergies, Rosemary would call Ann for dietary counseling. Sometimes, when the family was in search of employees to work at Crisp Acres, Rosemary would call Ann to see if she had any good applications.

"That's how I got to know her," Ann says. "We always had a friendly relationship, but it wasn't like we ran around together."

By the early1980s, hospitals nationwide were downsizing and trying to come up with ways to increase revenues in the face of a poor economy. After attending a conference, Marion Memorial's administrator called his management team together to discuss a new avenue hospitals were pursuing, which was focusing on health needs of women.

"He came out with that, and don't ask me why, I just thought 'I'm calling Rosemary,'" Ann says. "I told her about that meeting, and she talked about the health conferences she already was involved in, in Cape Girardeau, in Paducah, and elsewhere. She invited me over to show me some of the materials she had collected."

Ann then approached her boss at the hospital and said that Rosemary wanted to help.

"That just set the stage. Anybody who heard her name would go to any length to make something a success. We each chose eight or nine of our friends, met at the old Holiday Inn in Marion, and Rosemary got up and explained to them what a conference like this would be like."

If she had any doubts, Rosemary kept them to herself.

"When we first started the Women's Health Conference, people didn't know what it was about. We had to meet in individual homes, we would meet with local clubs, to just sell the idea of a women's health conference. I didn't think we could do this in the first year, but we were very determined that we could accomplish this."

They approached Ray Hancock, at the time the president of John A. Logan College in Carterville, about holding the inaugural conference there.

"He was delighted we were considering having the conference there," Ann recalls. "And Rosemary was thinking about where we would feed those attending. She said, 'Ray, what would you think if we used the gymnasium for our luncheon?' The man was close to falling off his chair, but he acted very calm. Because the gymnasium, of course, that was reserved for basketball. But Rosemary said we'd cover the floors. That's when I really became friends with her, because we worked so closely together. We respected each other; it was just a good relationship."

Ray – friends with Rosemary since junior high – chuckles at the memory of that first meeting.

"The problem was, for anybody who wanted to do a large event, the gymnasium was the only facility we had that was large enough. Later, we built facilities for those kinds of things. Rosemary was the first one who just insisted on having that luncheon there. But my concern was that you couldn't decorate it, you couldn't get the sound right, you could not make it look good. So that made the college look bad, and that made the event not come off the way people wanted it to. I was always extremely cautious about that; in fact, I didn't allow it very often – only on two occasions that I can remember. But Rosemary was very firm, and she knew how to handle Ray Hancock, and that's all there was to it. And she pulled it off."

The creation – and continuation – of the conference was "truly a labor of love," according to Rosemary. "It could never have been accomplished without the wonderful steering committees and all the volunteers."

Five years after that first conference, Rosemary, Ann and the other organizers began noticing a trend in the conference evaluation forms.

"We kept seeing from the parents and grandparents, 'Why don't you do something for the teens?'" Rosemary said. "We decided to have a Southern Illinois Women's Teen Conference. That has been successful, and it is still ongoing. We try to keep it health related, but we also have fun things for kids to do. We also introduce life skills, we talk about managing money or buying gifts for people without being so extravagant."

The teen conference, Ann says, was primarily Rosemary. "She always gave me credit, but she wanted to see that happen, what with five daughters. The first teen conference was held the same day as women's health. My thinking was, 'How in the world are we going to have a teen conference when we don't have the women's conference perfected?'"

Obviously, they succeeded. But they weren't done. These dedicated volunteers started getting requests for events more than once a year.

"We founded the Women's Educational Forum, where we would have speakers come in," Rosemary said. "Then we needed a parent company, so we formed Women for Health and Wellness Inc. The women's conference, the teen conference, the Women's Educational Forum are all

subsidiaries. We have done various style shows and other things for fundraising."

As if all of that isn't enough, there also is a conference for men, something that was – and remains important – to Ann.

"I always wanted to have a men's conference. And Rosemary gave her blessing and encouragement for that when she was very ill."

Twenty-five years later, the conferences still take place at the college. The 2008 Women's Health Conference was dedicated to Rosemary. Attendance at the 2009 conference numbered 543 women, a record and the maximum that the present location can accommodate.

Ann doesn't have one special memory of her good friend.

"For me, it is more of a collage of many different things about Rosemary, seeing how she handled many different situations. I saw her more in the way that she managed and handled things, because those were the things that really impressed me. They were learning experiences for me. At the health conference, she would always rehearse things, so they would be wonderful. One of the biggest things that impressed me was her conscientiousness. She was always striving for excellence, not accepting anything that could be done better."

Like Ann, Jo Poshard on many occasions saw firsthand what an "amazing lady" her good friend, Rosemary, was.

As with Ann, Jo's relationship with Rosemary also dated back some 30 years. Jo and husband Glenn, current president of Southern Illinois University, became acquainted with the Crisp family in the 1960s, when Glenn attended the university in Carbondale.

Glenn tended bar and bussed tables at Tony's restaurant on the Marion Square, and every weekend, Harry L.'s dad would come in for dinner and leave Glenn a $20 tip. Harry Sr. died in 1975, and when Glenn entered politics in the 1980s, the Poshards became better acquainted with Rosemary and Harry L. As Jo said, "Harry L. was the biggest businessman in all of Southern Illinois, and Glenn was one who would talk with Democrats, Republicans and independents, so the relationship developed even more." Over the years, the Poshards were frequent guests at Crisp family functions, and the friendship grew.

Rosemary's closest friends — Carmi Hill, Sue McCoskey and Marilyn Cavaness — gather at a luncheon.

When Jo retired in 2005 from her career as a teacher, Rosemary asked her to join the board of directors of Women's Health and Wellness. Advancing the status of women in Southern Illinois was one of Rosemary's visions, according to Jo, who continues to serve on the board.

She learned something new about her longtime friend shortly after joining the board.

"We were getting ready for the conference, and she always had a taste test of the luncheon food. The table was prepared, the food was brought in, and first we looked at the presentation, the color, the plates, where everything would be placed. I thought that was amazing; I had never seen this done the way she did this. In general, when you are planning an event, co-coordinators talk about choices, you make selections, you talk about colors and basically turn it over to the people catering the event."

Not Rosemary.

"The table was beautifully prepared," Jo recalls. "There was a detailed discussion about the presentation, and then the food came. There were discussions about the food. She always thought about the guests; she thought about what we would have for people with special needs. She said the

The Women's Health Conference advisory board: (Standing) Jo Poshard and Molly Norwood; (left to right) Dixie Travelstead, Fran Becque, Jo Sanders, Rosemary Crisp, Cathy Wood, Jill Cash and Janet Schuyler.

Rosemary's friends and colleagues: Sue McCoskey, Marilyn Cavaness, Yolande Peterson, Susan Phillips and Cathy Wood.

presentation is very important. That stuck with me. She wanted her home, her own appearance, she wanted what she did for others to be beautiful, to be lovely, so people would feel comfortable and pampered. She did it in some of the most unusual ways; for example, having the taste test. It mattered to her; the dishes, napkins, the centerpiece were all beautiful because she wanted her guests to enjoy it."

At the same time, presentation was only a part of the total package.

"When she said presentation is important, that was important in her life, her home and her appearance, but coupled with that was a very, very deep person," Jo emphasizes. "She wasn't a superficial person. She wanted a

good presentation, but it also was about the content. She wanted everything to be as good as it could be."

Serving others – her family, her friends, her community – was Rosemary's life.

"I know there was just something within Rosemary that allowed her to recognize her blessings and to want to share herself and the things she loved in life with other people. It's a gift that she had. As Rosemary was becoming more ill, she still would continue to do special things for all of us on the board. I would write her thank-you notes. And in those notes, I wanted her to know what a role model she was to me. I wanted to share that with her, so she'd know I felt that way about her. I had never seen such remarkable courage, such perseverance under tragic circumstances. She never stopped. I wanted her to know that I didn't know anybody else quite like her."

Jo, like Ann and so many others, learned much simply by watching Rosemary.

"One of the things that I really took away from Rosemary on a personal level is grace under pressure. That's an overly used phrase, but she really did exemplify that. She didn't talk about herself, about how bad she felt, about how many trips she made to the doctor. She would be honest about it, which I appreciated. She didn't try to cover up the fact that she was dealing with the cancer and how that was affecting her. But it was a matter of sharing it: 'This is what it is, and now, what are we going to do, what are we going to get done here today?' I thought that was amazing, that she didn't sit down and wait to be taken care of hand and foot. It would be unattainable to reach the level of grace and courage that Rosemary had. She would be my role model in aspiring to that."

So, too, was Rosemary a role model for her women's health conference co-founder.

"I saw this in action, it wasn't like I read it in a book or took a class," Ann says of Rosemary's commitment to family, to community, to all others. "It was just things that you know are the right way to be. You think to yourself, 'Surely no one practices this all the time.' I saw her in action. If I saw a bump in the road, I'd tell her, because I knew she would have an answer. Maybe it was

Rosemary tends to every detail at a Women's Health Conference.

a personality thing between us. I knew I could call her anyplace, anytime, and she'd never say 'I can't talk to you right now.'"

For Ann and the others who selflessly volunteer to make others' lives better, Rosemary's spirit lives on.

"We speak of her just as if she was off on a trip somewhere. There will never be another Rosemary. But we just feel that she is with us."

Jo also feels that spirit. "She would be very pleased that her work is carrying on. There is a lot of love from the people on the board, people want to do what Rosemary would wish them to do. They still want to please Rosemary, even now. She's just a presence; it's like she's there with us in the board room."

Creating Opportunities

Rosemary Crisp speaks at the dedication of Crisp Hall at Southeast Missouri State University.

'If you want to lift yourself up, lift up someone else.'

— Booker T. Washington, American educator

It really comes as no surprise that when Randy Dunn, a highly regarded educator, talks about Rosemary, he reflects on the lessons she taught for the many who knew and loved her – and the many who may not have had that pleasure but who nonetheless can continue to learn from her.

"She was a very humble person. I've always noted that there was this quality in her that may have been reflective of her Catholic upbringing and its role in her life, this notion of being a servant to others. When you truly take on that mane, it does cause one to be humble and think in terms of servant leadership. She was an amazing example of this."

Most of the soccer players and fans at Murray State University in Murray, Ky., where Randy serves as president, probably don't pay close attention to the name of the facility, the Rosemary and Harry L. Crisp II Soccer Complex. It does indeed reflect a gift Rosemary and Harry L. made to the university. But, as Randy knows, it wasn't a matter of having their name attached to something.

Randy Dunn, president of Murray State University, where a soccer complex is named after the Crisps.

"That isn't what motivates them. They came in, they didn't have a pet project or some monument they wanted to create. They said they had a general idea of an area they wanted to support, they asked what our needs were, and we presented some options we had developed. This was just a wonderful example of philanthropy on their part; it was the best response you want from major donors where they are simply looking forward to moving the institution forward."

Like his counterpart at Murray State, Ken Dobbins, president of Southeast Missouri State University in Cape Girardeau, where three of the six Crisp children attended, talks fondly about the couple's generosity. Yes, Rosemary and Harry L. have been strong financial supporters of the university. But what Ken

likes to emphasize is generosity of spirit, a commitment to others. Rosemary, he says, was a very special person.

"When you look at what she was able to do in the later years of her life when she was afflicted with so much pain and disease, she stood up to that and survived for many, many years. She just had a constitution that would make her a survivor. Even when fighting that personally, she cared about students and was very giving of her time, talent and treasures to make sure she could leave the world, the organization or the university in a better position."

The Rosemary Berkel Crisp Hall of Nursing at Southeast reflects her passion for nursing and for helping others. It houses many of the College of Health and Human Services' academic departments, including, of course, nursing. Rosemary visited the campus in the last few weeks before she died.

"The nursing program was near and dear to her heart," Ken recalls. "She was on the advisory board, she kept in contact with many of our faculty members, and she would come and visit from time to time. We needed the money to renovate some classrooms in that facility so our nursing program could get accredited. The Crisps were instrumental in that."

They also were instrumental in the establishment of the Rosemary Berkel and Harry L. Crisp II Southeast Missouri Regional Museum, which opened at Southeast's River Campus in the fall of 2007. The 14,000-square-foot facility, featuring more than 5,900-square-feet of exhibition space, attracts people from throughout the region with its focus on the archaeology, history and fine arts of Southeast Missouri.

Ken also enjoys telling the story of how a business decision to close down a plant in fact opened new doors of opportunity.

After operating a plant in Malden for many years, Harry L. and his team made a business decision to close the plant. Together with Southeast's administration at that time, they had a dream to create a higher education center.

"We're the only four-year institution in 24 counties, and the nearest community college is an hour-and-a-half north and an hour-and-a-half west," Ken explains. "For Malden, Pepsi was a big employer. When they closed, the Crisps wanted to make sure they could give back to the community. So, they gave us the land, and community members raised money, and we built classrooms inside that Pepsi plant."

The Harry L. Crisp Bootheel Education Center – named for Harry L.'s dad – started with an office and four or five classrooms. Now called Southeast Missouri State University-Malden, the facility includes 18 classrooms, nine offices, a library and other amenities.

"For them to provide the building, that gave encouragement to the citizens of Malden to donate for classrooms and for scholarships so their kids could go there," Ken says. Since the concept first took flight 23 years ago, Southeast has received more than $4.7 million in donations.

The 275 students who attend the education center take freshman and sophomore courses, then transfer to Southeast in Cape Girardeau to finish their undergraduate work. The Malden center also offers bachelor's degrees in several education majors.

"Those students would have to travel more than an hour to Poplar Bluff to go to school," Ken says. "We

Kenneth Dobbins, president of Southeast Missouri State University.

have lots of place-bound students who wouldn't have gone on to higher education without that center. That model was recognized nationally in higher education. We used that model at Malden to build three other regional campuses, in Kennett, in Sikeston and in Perryville. So, we now have almost 1,600 students, and it all started with that model.

"If it wasn't for the Crisp family, I don't know that that would have happened. You talk about the number of students at Malden and the other regional campuses, it has made a difference in many, many lives."

Rosemary and Harry L. "truly want to make sure others have an opportunity to get an education. They see that just like I do, education is the difference-maker."

Both were charter members of Southeast's foundation Board of Directors, and both received the foundation's highest honor as "Friends of the University" – Rosemary

Nursing school dedicates Crisp Hall

Crisp

The nursing unit at Southeast Missouri State University in Cape Girardeau has been named Crisp Hall to recognize the personal and financial dedication of Rosemary Crisp of Marion.

Crisp, along with her husband, Harry Crisp II, owners of the Marion Pepsi-Cola Bottling Co., provided a six-figure gift for renovation of the unit and construction of a 13,000-square-foot addition.

Crisp serves on the university's department of nursing renovation advisory board.

Crisp is a graduate of the St. Mary's Hospital School of Nursing in Evansville. She is a registered nurse, a member of the 14th District of the Illinois Nursing Association, board member of the National League for Nursing Community Health Accreditation Program in New York and co-chairperson for the Southern Illinois Women's Health Conference.

A formal dedication ceremony was held at Crisp Hall on Oct. 21.

DEDICATION OF CRISP HALL

On October 21, 1988 on the campus of Southeast Missouri State University, Rosemary Crisp was honored with the dedication of the hall of nursing being named Rosemary Berkel Crisp Hall of Nursing, or Crisp Hall for short.

Mrs. Crisp, a member of the Copper Dome Society of Southeast Missouri State, as well as recipient of the "Friend of the University" award in 1986, has received this honor for her personal and financial commitment for the advancement of nursing at the university.

The renovation of Crisp Hall includes a 13,000 square foot addition and a new entry plaza on the south side of the 1922 structure. The addition contains a new nursing skills laboratory, a new nursing assessment lab, classrooms, conference rooms, and the center for health and counseling, which houses the university's health and counseling services for faculty, staff and students.

The keynote speaker for the dedication was Pam Maraldo, Ph.D., chief executive officer of the National League for Nursing (NLN).

Bob Mees, Harry L. and Rosemary look at a display cabinet dedicated to the Crisp family for their contributions to John A. Logan College, of which Mees is president. Harry L. and Rosemary are known for their support of community colleges and universities.

Rosemary stands in front of the Rosemary Berkel Crisp Hall of Nursing at SEMO in Cape Girardeau.

The Crisps also support medical research and care, including the Mayo Clinic in Rochester, Minn. The family was joined by Mayo Clinic physicians for this photo. Included are (front row) Carole, Harry L., Rosemary and Cathy; (middle row) Cara, Harry 'Lee,' Dr. Brigitte Barrette (Rosemary's physician), Cyndi and Dr. Kelly; (back row) Brice Deschamps-Barrette, Dr. Robert B. Diasio (Mayo Clinic Cancer Center Director) and Dr. Claude Deschamps.

Jim Henderson of Culver Academies presents Rosemary with an honorary ring from the school. Rosemary is only the second woman to become an honorary graduate of Culver Academies.

Rosemary Crisp was a general trustee of
The Lincoln Academy of Illinois.

With Rosemary at his side, Harry L. organized the Illinois Community College System Foundation. Former Gov. Jim Edgar was the keynote speaker when the two-story building that houses the foundation staff in Springfield was dedicated in 1999 as the Harry L. Crisp II Community College Center. Eleven years later, two additional floors were added.

Bob Mees, president of Logan College, knows how important Rosemary and Harry L.'s support, including advocacy for his institution and the community college system in general, has been. A room in the college's conference center bears Harry L.'s name, and Rosemary was intimately involved in the creation of a statue of her husband, right down to the lapel pin. Nearby, a display recognizes the entire family, and a plaque specifically honors Rosemary.

He also deeply appreciates Rosemary's vision that led to her co-founding the Southern Illinois Women's Health Conference and Women's Teen Conference. Not only does the college host the annual events, which now include a men's health conference, it provides office space for the umbrella organization Women for Health and Wellness Inc.

"Rosemary was compassionate, considerate of everybody else, charismatic, dedicated, innovative, and most importantly, she was an inspiration," Bob said. "She was so passionate about everything she did."

For Harry L., it goes back to what Randy Dunn says about a spirit of generosity.

"Both of us enjoy what we've accomplished, and we enjoy sharing it. When we can see that we have made a small impression to better things in society, that's very rewarding to both of us. That is where we devoted our life. I was the chair of the Illinois Community College System, and the great thing about our effort was that it gave people an opportunity to help themselves. There's nothing more you can do for people than to give them an opportunity."

in 1986 and Harry L. in 2005. Rosemary also was the first chair of the President's Council, serving in the role for more than a decade, and both are charter members of the group, the foundation's organization that recognizes major donors.

"They are two of the most generous individuals I've ever known, and I don't just mean in terms of money," Ken says. "I'm talking about their time, their talents and contributing to the organization, whatever organization they are in; they're not just members, they're participating members, and that organization will be better."

Their support of education has been wide-ranging and has included critical gifts to John A. Logan College in Carterville and Southern Illinois University Carbondale, among others. Harry L. was a founding board member of Logan College, and was even involved, with others, in selecting the name.

Enduring Friendships

Rosemary is flanked by lifelong friends Marilyn Cavaness, Sue McCoskey and Carmi Hill, all of Marion.

'She thought the whole world was her neighborhood.'

— Father Richard Mohr

Rosemary regularly had lunch with good friends, and this photo was taken at Bennie's in Marion. They are Marilyn Cavaness, Sue McCoskey, Carmi Hill, Carole, Rosemary, Ruth Hancock and Lou Ann Sims.

*T*hat's how Father Rich, Rosemary's longtime priest at St. Joseph's Catholic Church in Marion and close family friend, describes her unique ability to forge deep connections with so many people. Her friendships in that vast neighborhood were so meaningful for a very simple reason: She cared. Rosemary always put others before herself.

Her daughters marvel at how often people would approach them and say, "Your mom and I are close friends." Whether she was serving with them on a board in Washington, D.C., or helping with a Girl Scout troop, Rosemary connected with those around her.

When Marilyn Cavaness, Sue McCoskey and Carmi Hill got together to reminisce about Rosemary, there was plenty of conversation, with no shortage of laughter and tears.

That's to be expected among a group of women who share, literally, a lifetime of memories. These three Marion women trace their friendship with Rosemary to the time she was dating Harry L. And how they miss her.

"We wish we could clone her," Sue says.

Together, they celebrated each other's special occasions and joys, and offered comfort and consolation when life took a difficult turn. For half a century, their lives were inextricably linked.

When they all started out as young marrieds with little ones, they – and other friends as well – often spent beautiful Sundays relaxing at area parks, such as Ferne Clyffe or Giant City, or at a lake where they could share a boat. Together, they'd push the youngsters in their strollers or simply enjoy each other's company while the little ones played in their playpens. On weekends, everyone brought their own meat and a dish to share for cookouts. After Rosemary and Harry L. built their home at Lake of Egypt, south of Marion, they frequently hosted those Sunday gatherings "for a long, long, long time," Marilyn recalled.

Wednesdays also were special in those early days. That's when the husbands had their night at the Elks Club. The ladies, with children in tow, would gather at someone's apartment or home for dinner and conversation.

The four women shared much throughout the years. They belonged to the Gamba Lamba Beta Chapter of Delta Theta Tau Sorority, a national women's organization devoted to philanthropy and charity. Sue smiles as she remembers a trip she and Carmi took to visit the Crisps at their condo in Ocean Reef, Fla. Rosemary always introduced them to friends there as her sorority sisters.

For the last 25 years of Rosemary's life, the women were part of a birthday club that continues to meet, even now. Each month, the 20 or so members get together to celebrate the members' birthdays that fall during that month. And there was the monthly meeting of the Pinochle club. In between, there were informal lunches and get-togethers.

With her often-hectic schedule, Rosemary couldn't always participate. But even when travels took her far from Marion, her friends were always in her heart. Sue laughs as she remembers a trip from many years ago that Rosemary and Harry L. took.

"I think it might have been the Philippines. I don't know how many pairs of shoes she brought back for all of her friends. She called us over, and she had them on a ping pong table. I'll bet there were 50 or 60 pairs of shoes, and we all just picked the colors and sizes we wanted."

"We thought we were something special to have those shoes, especially at that time," Marilyn chimed in. "Way back then, we were relatively young marrieds with young children, just starting out."

It never surprised the women that their dear friend was so adept at balancing the many facets of her life.

"She was organized, and she was a planner," Sue says. "I had a dress shop for many years, Stylart, and Rosemary shopped there. It was a family tradition that they shopped with us. At Christmas time, she would come in with this yellow pad with the names of all these people she would

be buying for. She conquered all that organizing through planning ahead of time. She had gifts for people in Florida, gifts for people in Marion, for business people and for all of her friends."

Carmi and Rosemary shared, among many things, a love of art – Rosemary was an accomplished painter – and found that they had very similar tastes. Rosemary relied on Carmi's help year after year in getting ready for the Women's Health Conference. Together on committees, they would craft the centerpieces at Carmi's house and decorate in advance of the annual gathering.

All three women, like so many others, continue to marvel at the strength, courage and grace Rosemary displayed throughout her illness. No matter how she might have felt, her focus always was on others. Marilyn remembered undergoing ankle surgery at a time when Rosemary was at Mayo Clinic for a procedure. Rosemary called to check on her.

"I can't tell you how much I've always appreciated how kind Rosemary has been through all of my illnesses," Marilyn said. "Because even though she was so ill herself, she would always be very caring of me, trying to see that I was comfortable and able to go someplace."

The fact of the matter is that they drew strength from each other. Rosemary completely understood the health challenges Marilyn faced.

"I have to look up to her. She is in pain a lot of days, and she tries to keep her chin up. Whenever I have traveled or had special events, she would always call and want to hear about them. We've had good days, we've had tough days, we try to keep each other positive and get out and do things."

Rosemary's focus always was on living. "She did everything to keep from being defeated, and Harry L. helped her in every way," Marilyn added.

Carmi often sat with Rosemary during chemo treatments at the Marion hospital.

"One time, she got done with her chemo treatment, they unhooked her, and she said, 'Well, Carmi, let's go shopping.' She went right from the hospital to the mall."

No matter what each day brought, Rosemary knew she could always count on her "neighborhood."

"My personal friends, if I needed them to come to the hospital, or to the house to sit with me, they'd always do

Rosemary loved art and was an accomplished painter. The photo at right is a framed painting by Rosemary.

that. After having chemo, if I didn't feel like getting up off the sofa, they would do that, talk quietly and enjoy each other's company. That has been very supportive."

Anytime Rosemary traveled to Mayo, her lifelong friends would call each day to check on her.

"We then would share it with all the others in our birthday club, the sorority, the Pinochle club," Marilyn recalled. "Everyone worried about her."

That's because they all looked after each other. Rosemary was very loyal to all of her friends, no matter where they lived.

"She brought us together," Marilyn said.

And she would bring them together one final time. On Dec. 1, 2007, the family continued to hold vigil at Rosemary's bedside in Marion Memorial Hospital, as they had been doing for days. Hospice volunteers advised the family that the end was near.

"We waited and waited, not wanting to leave her," daughter Cara recalls. "Mom would take deep breaths, but minutes, hours went by. Then her three friends, Marilyn, Sue and Carmi, came to visit her. They were reluctant to come in Mom's room, afraid they would be intruding. But we encouraged them, and they came in and talked quietly with Mom. Then, Mom passed away. Her family and her dearest friends were with her. She was at peace."

Brenda Edgar, former First Lady of Illinois, isn't sure Rosemary realized the impact she had on people just by being herself. She attracted people because, Brenda says, "there was a naturalness about her."

"Despite our busy schedules, Rosemary was the kind of person that even though we might not see her for six months or a year, we would just pick up right where we left off. It was that kind of friendship, a mutual understanding of one another's lives, and the time that was available. We really enjoyed being together. I know there was a real deep understanding between both of us about expectations and responsibilities. We understood the going-all-the-time, here, there and everywhere."

And go she did, cancer and all.

"She handled her cancer with great strength, dignity, almost with humor," Brenda recalls. "She would tell the story about taking a cruise, even with all of the things she needed to have with her, they'd just go. When a bag of IV fluid that she had to have was empty, she'd toss it in the trash and go on. Others, by that time, would have the covers over their head. You would hope to have that kind of inner strength, know that it's possible, because she showed us how possible it is."

Brenda has many "lovely memories" of Rosemary, noting that she frequently celebrated happy birthdays with her. Brenda's birthday is at the end of August, so it always coincided with the Du Quoin State Fair, which she attended over the years with her husband, former Gov. Jim Edgar. For Rosemary and Harry L., the fair was an annual tradition.

She also enjoys her memories of spending time with Rosemary during a Republican National Convention in New York City.

"She gave me a little bear with the Statue of Liberty," Brenda recalls. "I still have that, and when I look at it, it reminds me of how thoughtful she was. She was always taking pictures. She was enjoying life and she wanted others to enjoy life, she wanted to share the beauty of every minute. During that trip to New York, everywhere I'd go, there she'd be. I just didn't understand how she did it, looking like a picture of health, and, of course, she wasn't, but you wouldn't have known it. It just puzzled me how she kept going."

Of course, as Brenda and so many others in that large "neighborhood" knew, Rosemary drew an enormous amount of strength from her faith.

"I had encouraged her to write a book, and one of the reasons was because I wanted to know, people wanted to know, how she maintained her composure," Brenda says. "She always was so positive and upbeat in the midst of everything she was going through with her illness. I wanted her to say, 'This is how I do it.' I don't think she realized how she amazed people. She could be with a group of people, dealing with some of the side effects of her health, and nobody would have known. I was just awed by that thought after I learned about some of what she was dealing with. You could be with her and never have known any of the medical history."

To this day, Janet Albers, who lives in Dallas, continues to marvel at the positive attitude, strength and spirit she saw during many trips with Rosemary and Harry L. Like Harry

Rosemary and her good friend, Marilyn Cavaness.

L., Janet's husband, John – who passed away 10 months after Rosemary – was in the soft drink business, and that connection brought the couples together in the early 1990s.

"She handled her cancer with a total positive reaction," Janet says. "I didn't know her when she first had cancer a long time ago. She told me that she made a deal with God, that if she could get through that first bout so she could raise her children, then she would accept whatever came. She won most of her bouts with her positive attitude. It never kept her from doing anything. She kept on going forward, she kept on accomplishing things, taking care of her family, her husband, the projects she was involved with."

One of Janet's favorite memories was the last trip she and her husband took with the Crisps, a cruise on the Mediterranean Sea. While Harry L. certainly enjoyed their trips, he preferred staying back to do what he enjoyed while the others went sightseeing.

"My husband, Rosemary and I would go out for the day, whether it was Monte Carlo, Rome, wherever it was, the three of us would go sightseeing all day. When we would get into Monte Carlo, we would walk up to the city, and Rosemary would tell us that we needed to sit down in a coffee shop where she could do a 'transfer' – I think it was saline to clean out her system. Most people, myself included, would have been in the hospital saying, 'OK, nurses, you take care of this.' Not Rosemary. She was cruising the Mediterranean, transferring the bottles of saline. We'd sit and have a cup of coffee while she was doing that, then we would go on with our sightseeing. She might take a little bit of a rest, and then she was ready to go to dinner and do whatever was available. She never stopped doing anything."

Janet and John loved to travel, to shop, to sightsee. "But we were barely keeping up with Rosemary, no matter how sick she was. Even with her illness, she had just as much energy. She was an ideal for all of us."

Janet laughs at the memory of a trip they all took to Australia, which included a high-speed boat trip on a river.

"Rosemary had been having chemo treatments, of course. She had lost her hair and was wearing a wig. For this boat trip, you have to put on rubber suits, headgear and goggles, and the boat ride lasts maybe 20 to 30 minutes. We get to the end, and we're all still in our suits talking about it. One of the guys looks at Rosemary and notices she's got this thing at her feet – it looked like some kind of wild animal. So she looks down and says, 'Oh, it's just my wig. I took it off and put it in my suit.' She didn't care."

That simply was Rosemary, completely comfortable with who she was.

"She was as comfortable shopping, living, doing in Marion as she was in New York, Paris or Hong Kong," Janet says. "She was the very same person no matter what she did. She just had so many talents."

Janet describes Rosemary as totally selfless.

"Of course, she was a very strong Catholic, a believing person who had her ideals in life set straight early on, and she didn't vary from those. She loved people, she loved her family. I don't think I ever saw her disappointed in anyone or anything. I know there are other women in history who have love for their family and friends, but she also had a strong business sense to her. She could get into various nonprofits or her church and offer very strong advice. She was a great woman, a woman to emulate."

Like Brenda and Jim Edgar, former Illinois First Lady Lura Lynn Ryan and her husband, former Gov. George Ryan, also loved the times they spent at the Du Quoin fair with Rosemary and Harry L. They all had become good friends long before her husband became governor, and it is a friendship that Lura Lynn treasured.

"I have met many, many lovely people, but she was a sweetheart, just a dear. She had a very positive attitude. She was always concerned about everyone else, making sure that everyone was doing all right. Some people are just born that way. I've always been a very positive person. So was Rosemary, that's why we got along so well."

That positive nature was a source of inspiration to good friend Molly Norwood, herself a breast cancer survivor. Rosemary, in fact, was among the first people in whom Molly confided. Molly and her husband, Bill, were attending an event at Southern Illinois University in Carbondale shortly after Molly had received her diagnosis.

"Rosemary and Harry L. were there, and I shared this news with her. I knew what she had been going through, so I shared this with her. She said, 'You will get a second opinion, won't you? You will go to Mayo Clinic, won't you?'

This group was known as the Fearless Foursome. Each couple planned a different trip each year, and they traveled the world for many years. They are (from left) Gerald and Suzanne McGuire, John and Janet Albers, Rosemary and Harry L., and Rose Marie and James Lee.

And I said 'Yes.' She offered any help they could provide, including flying us up to Mayo. We had already made our arrangements. But I remember that moment, and I remember after that her constant diligence, her concern, staying in contact, and so that drew us into a closer relationship."

The Rosemary whom Molly knew was the same woman everyone knew: Gentle, kind, wise, humble.

"She never saw herself as powerful or as someone who's above people. I remember seeing Rosemary come out of Kohl's Department Store with carts of things for her kids for Christmas, and she was so excited because it was senior citizen's day. I can remember when she discovered the Big Lots store. She did not see herself as any different than anyone else. She came from very humble beginnings. She never forgot that."

As is often the case among close friends, simple, every-day occurrences become special memories. One such memory for Molly is a 2006 shopping trip in Arizona, where she and Bill spent the winters. Rosemary and Harry L. were in town to attend a banquet where Harry L. was being honored.

"I met her at a mall and we shopped. We were hungry, but we didn't want to have a big lunch because we knew we had the big awards dinner that night. So we went in the food court and got greasy burgers and greasy, greasy fries. We sat there eating all of this greasy food, and Rosemary ate everything. We had our fill of grease that day and laughed and laughed, and it was such a good day."

It was a special moment, a simple moment that reflected Rosemary's determination to enjoy all that life had to offer.

"All of the things people will say about Rosemary will be because of what was in her heart. Her beauty in handling all of this gave you strength. It made you want to do better. It made you realize you have nothing to complain about. She made you think the world is beautiful and you never felt sorry for her. You only felt happiness for her. The only mourning I do is for myself, not for her, but for my loss. Because she is happy, believe me."

With a friendship that stretches back to the early 1960s, Mabel and Jim Foreman also know firsthand of Rosemary and Harry L.'s compassion and loyalty. In 1971, Jim – now

retired after a distinguished career as a federal judge in Southern Illinois – underwent his first heart bypass surgery at Barnes-Jewish Hospital in St. Louis.

"Harry L. called me after we got Jim home and asked me what we were doing back in Southern Illinois," Mabel says. "He said, 'You get on that plane and come down to Florida.' They were very gracious, very unselfish, very kind."

That was the Foremans' introduction to Ocean Reef, and they subsequently purchased a condo there because of Rosemary and Harry L.

"We had a wonderful relationship, a good friendship," Mabel said. "With the four of us, I felt we could ask the other for anything, anytime."

If there was one word to describe Rosemary, Mabel said it would be "graciousness." Added her husband: "I don't think I can improve on that. Graciousness suggests dignity, and that applies to Rosemary."

The couples spent a great deal of time together, particularly throughout Rosemary's illness.

"I've known a lot of cancer patients," Mabel says, noting that she is a breast cancer survivor. "Rosemary was one who, if she was in the hospital let's say on Thursday, and she wanted to go shopping on Friday, she was dressed and gone. She never let anything stop her. I've never known anybody like her, truly. She is an inspiration."

Ray Hancock knew from the time he attended Washington Junior High School in Marion with Rosemary that his friend was someone special. As he says, he was able to watch her "really blossom into a beautiful woman with a great personality" in high school.

"Harry L. got awful lucky," he says, smiling.

After high school, Ray and Rosemary went their separate ways – he served in the Navy, she went to nursing school. But they both returned to Southern Illinois, and over the ensuing years, Ray and his wife, Ruth, remained casual friends with Rosemary and Harry L., Ruth and Rosemary shared membership in the Delta Theta Tau sorority, which Ruth joined in the mid-1960s.

In fact, Rosemary hosted Ruth's initiation party at the Crisps' home, and as Ruth says, "That was the first of many gatherings as a sorority sister and friend." And while Ruth described the Crisps' home as one of the larger ones

The Fearless Foursome wives: Rose Marie, Janet, Rosemary and Suzanne.

Three of the Fearless Foursome: Rosemary and Harry L., Janet and John, Suzanne and Gerald.

she had been to, "Rosemary frequently talked just like the rest of the girls about a tight budget raising kids. She too had limits on spending money on clothes. We all used to pass around clothes when our kids outgrew them."

Higher education would eventually bring the four closer together.

Harry L. was a charter board member of John A. Logan College in Carterville, serving as a trustee from 1967 to 1971. Ray, meanwhile, joined the college in 1974 as an academic dean. He would go on to hold several other positions and, in 1989, he became college president. At about that time, James Thompson, then governor of Illinois, named Harry L. chairman of the Illinois Community College Board.

"All of a sudden," Ray says, "there was a very strong connection again between Harry L. and Rosemary and Ruth and me."

There also was a family connection. In 1986, Rosemary's niece, Colleen, married the Hancocks' son, Daryl. Colleen's close cousin, Cheryl Crisp, was the maid of honor.

"Whenever Rosemary made trips to the many countries they visited on business over the years, she would include my daughter-in-law when buying dolls for her own girls," Ruth relates. "It is a beautiful collection of international dolls."

She credits Rosemary with "giving me another start in life," after Ruth suffered a major heart attack while she and Ray were visiting their son in Virginia in 1995. As they tell the emotional story, they pause often, because as Ray says, "We didn't know if Ruth was going to make it."

Ray well remembers the phone call from Rosemary the morning after Ruth's heart attack, offering encouragement and help of any kind.

"She said, 'I just want you to listen to me. This is a subject I know more about than you do. You're having a bad time right now, but when she comes out of this, you're going to have a real problem.' I asked what she meant, and she said, 'I'll tell you when it gets closer.'"

Finally, the doctors said Ruth could leave the hospital and return home to Illinois. But they said she couldn't fly commercial, and she couldn't ride in a car.

"I suddenly realized, and I called Rosemary and said, 'OK, I've got the problem, what's the solution?' She asked when we wanted to come home, I told her anytime, and she told me to give her a day, and they would send their airplane for us."

When Ruth was able to talk on the phone, Rosemary was the first person she spoke with outside of family. She knew that Rosemary, with her nursing skills, would be able to answer her questions.

"That's when she told me about a small problem she had found, but that she was assured by the doctor it could wait until January when she returned from a trip they had planned. Of course, that was the beginning of her problems, which lasted 12 years.

"It was her encouragement to me then and over those years that really showed me that she was my angel."

Rosemary also had many special angels in her life throughout those 12 years. A remarkable doctor at the Mayo Clinic held a special place in her heart.

Rosemary and Ray Hancock, a retired John A. Logan College president, became friends in junior high school. Ray and his wife, Ruth, were among the many people who celebrated Rosemary's 60th birthday in 1997.

Doctor, Friend, Confidante

Dr. Brigitte Barrette, Rosemary's Mayo Clinic physician, says Rosemary was the perfect patient. 'Whatever I asked, she would just do it. She was very determined to do whatever was needed to live. I would explain something, and Rosemary would understand, because of her nursing background.'

'When I am your doctor, I try to imagine
the kind of doctor I'd like if I were you.
Then I try to be that kind of doctor.'

— Charles W. Mayo,
American physician
and co-founder of Mayo Clinic

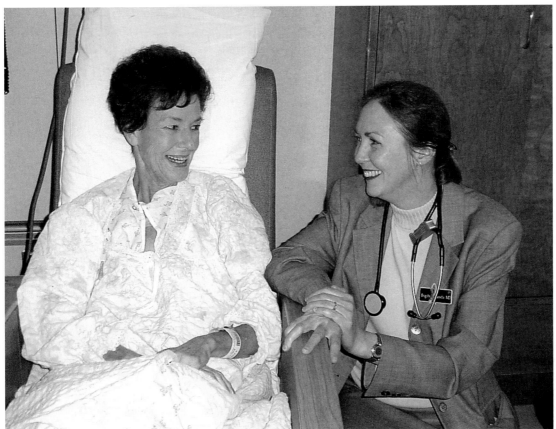

Rosemary and Dr. Barrette were not only medical partners; they became good friends.

A lecture hall at the Mayo Clinic in Rochester, Minn., will forever serve as a tribute to the kindness and selflessness of Rosemary Crisp.

There's still a hint of amazement in her voice as Dr. Brigitte A. Barrette, assistant professor and consultant in gynecology and oncology at Mayo, shares the memory. She was Rosemary's physician and very close friend for 12 years.

At a luncheon in June 2007, Mayo honored Rosemary and Harry L. for their generosity in establishing the Rosemary Berkel Crisp, R.N., and Harry L. Crisp II Endowment for Research in Female Cancers. The support of Mayo and its cancer research led the clinic to name a lecture hall in Rosemary's honor. But, in a heartfelt gesture to her physician and friend, Rosemary made sure that the name is "Rosemary Berkel Crisp Lecture Hall Honoring Brigitte A. Barrette." Honored as she was by that gesture, the doctor was totally taken aback by an announcement at the luncheon.

"We had this lunch, with her entire family there, so we could say thank you to them. But I knew she had something in mind. Rosemary made an arrangement because she really wanted to 'do something' for me. When I retire, they will switch the names, so it will be the Brigitte A. Barrette Lecture Hall Honoring Rosemary Berkel Crisp."

That, Dr. Barrette says, was a complete surprise, because it is something that just isn't done very often at Mayo.

"Even now, people talk to me about it when they see that lecture hall honoring me. It was just amazing. Physicians who work at Mayo, if they are looking for a lot of money or honors or power, it probably isn't the place for them. Our motto is that the needs of the patient come first, so ours is more of a humble role."

Rosemary was the perfect patient.

"Whatever I asked, she would just do it. She was very determined to do whatever was needed to live. I would explain something, and Rosemary would understand, because of her nursing background."

Their relationship clearly transcended the traditional roles of doctor and patient.

"I treated her for 12 years, and that's a significant amount of time. But over that time, I also just got very close to Rosemary because we had a lot of similarities. We would have long discussions about things other than illness, such as religion, as we are both Catholic. But she was one of the only people I knew who would understand when I talked about something, because either she went through those things or she was more aware of business things."

Dr. Barrette and her husband, Dr. Claude Deschamps, often were guests of the Crisps at their Ocean Reef, Fla., condo; to this day, they continue to spend time there with Harry L. and family members. And the trips Rosemary and Harry L. took to Minnesota weren't always devoted to health matters.

"There was such kindness to her. There was no question she would put her attention toward you and was genuinely interested in you. At the time, I was president of a choir here, and they came to one of our benefit dinners," Dr. Barrette recalls. "They didn't have to do that. In fact they came to a few of our concerts. I know she liked it, but she could have done many other things. She just was very attentive. She came to my house a few times, and she treated it like it was a major event for her. She really was so happy to come. They came for dinner a few times; once it was just to sit and talk in the screened-in porch. She was so grateful. And that's more than her nursing background. That was her personality."

Rosemary always sent gifts at Christmas. And when Dr. Barrette's husband became chair of the surgery department at Mayo, Rosemary and Harry L. sent flowers.

"She was happy for us. This was just her," Dr. Barrette says fondly.

During one of the trips to Florida, Rosemary and Harry L. introduced Dr. Barrette to one of their friends who was on the board of directors of the Westminster Dog Show. That was a treat for the doctor, who is a dog lover. The two couples later got tickets for the show.

"Unfortunately, the year we had the tickets to go, Rosemary got sick. But my husband and I and Harry L. went to the dog show this year, and that was to honor her, because of how much she had wanted to go."

When she thinks about her friend, Dr. Barrette thinks about grace.

"Rosemary was a graceful individual, there is no question about that. There was grace in her behavior, in her always thinking of wanting to do good.

"Rosemary was very rare."

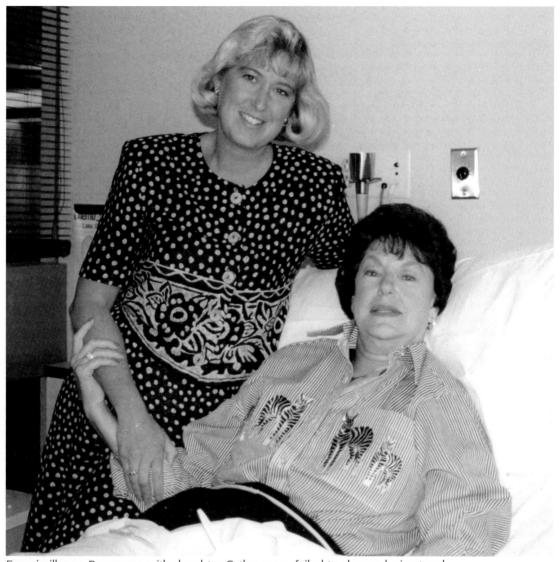

Even in illness, Rosemary, with daughter Cathy, never failed to share a loving touch.

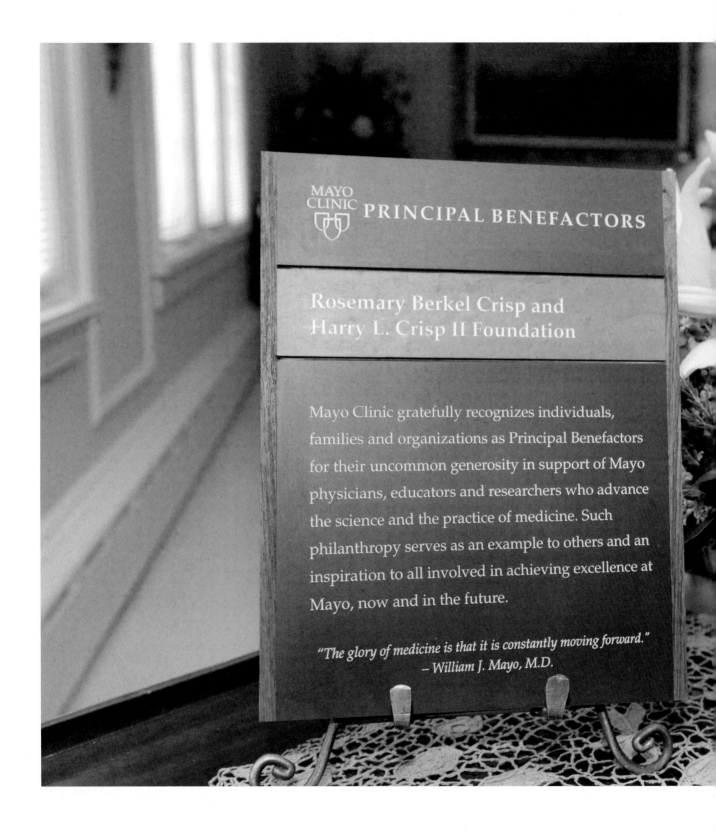

MAYO CLINIC **PRINCIPAL BENEFACTORS**

Rosemary Berkel Crisp and Harry L. Crisp II Foundation

Mayo Clinic gratefully recognizes individuals, families and organizations as Principal Benefactors for their uncommon generosity in support of Mayo physicians, educators and researchers who advance the science and the practice of medicine. Such philanthropy serves as an example to others and an inspiration to all involved in achieving excellence at Mayo, now and in the future.

"The glory of medicine is that it is constantly moving forward."
— William J. Mayo, M.D.

A plaque commemorates the Rosemary Berkel Crisp, R.N., and Harry L. Crisp II Endowment for Research in Female Cancers at Mayo Clinic in Rochester, Minn. When Rosemary's physician retires, a lecture hall, now called the Rosemary Berkel Crisp Lecture Hall Honoring Brigitte A. Barrette, will be known as the Brigitte A. Barrette Lecture Hall Honoring Rosemary Berkel Crisp. The change in name was requested by Rosemary to honor her physician and friend.

An Inspiring Woman

Rosemary Crisp was an honoree at the 2007 Inspiring Women Banquet at Southern Illinois University.

'Don't say you don't have enough time.
You have exactly the same number of hours
per day that were given to Helen Keller,
Pasteur, Michelangelo, Mother Teresa,
Leonardo da Vinci, Thomas Jefferson
and Albert Einstein.'

— H. Jackson Brown Jr.,
American author,
'Life's Little Instruction Book'

When Rosemary received an Inspiring Women award at Southern Illinois University in Carbondale in 2007, many in the audience of hundreds were unaware of just how far her illness had progressed. What they were aware of, however, was her remarkable dedication to improving the lives of the region's residents. Rosemary didn't seek awards or the spotlight; she was driven by a sense of social responsibility.

Many of those who nominated Rosemary spoke of her commitment to health care. As a volunteer nurse, she served at Red Cross blood drives, as a glaucoma screener for the Lions Club, and, of course, at Girl Scout camp. While certainly well-known for the Women for Health and Wellness conferences that she co-founded, Rosemary volunteered her time in so many other ways, including on the board of the Hands of Hope Clinic in Marion and the Marion Memorial Hospital Auxiliary Board.

Her efforts extended well beyond Southern Illinois. Joan Shaver, from the University of Illinois-Chicago College of Nursing, served with Rosemary on the advisory council for the National Institute of Nursing Research at the National Institutes of Health, the governmental agency that funds the vast majority of health science research in the United States. Tommy Thompson, then Secretary of Health and Human Services, named Rosemary to the council in 2003, an appointment she was especially proud of. It provided her with yet another opportunity, this time at the national level, to serve as a health-care advocate.

"Rosemary, a nurse but not a researcher, provided the voice of the public as we processed the agenda and strategic plans of the NINR," Dr. Shaver wrote in her nomination letter. "The perspectives that she presented grounded the council discussions in the reality of circumstances for the beneficiaries of health science research. She performed her advisory council role with sophistication, clarity and admirable articulation."

The Inspiring Women awards committee also heard from Dr. Brigitte Barette, who wrote that she had the "privilege" of serving as Rosemary's physician at the Mayo Clinic since 1986. Dr. Barrette mentioned that Rosemary

Rosemary is radiant during her speech at the October banquet. She passed away two months later.

and Harry L. had made a very generous donation to Mayo for female cancer research.

But she also wanted the committee to know that Rosemary was the main benefactor at a benefit dinner for the Choral Arts Ensemble, a choir in Rochester, Minn.

In 2009, Dr. Barrette made a donation to Inspiring Women in honor of her longtime patient and very close friend.

Perhaps this observation, included in one of the letters of nomination, best describes Rosemary's guiding philosophy: "She has given so much more than she will ever receive."

Rosemary was photographed in her home, Crisp Acres, for the Inspiring Women banquet. One of the letters of nomination for the Inspiring Women award said, 'She has given so much more than she will ever receive.'

The following is Rosemary's speech at the 2007 Inspiring Women's Banquet:

After thanking and recognizing colleagues, family and friends, Rosemary began:

My background is from very humble beginnings. My father had only a third-grade formal education, due to his mother dying in childbirth. He was sent from Equality to Eldorado, from family to family. Later in life, he learned the trade of welding and was excellent in his field.

My mother and dad were married over 50 years and had four children. I'm the youngest. I credit my parents with the strong family values and closeness we cherish today.

We were all given the opportunity to go to college. My two older sisters were secretaries, and my brother and I decided to further our college education, Jim as a mechanical engineer and me as a nurse.

In our family, there was a lot of love, faith in God, and family and friends around. We were taught to take personal responsibility, honesty and integrity.

Being open to opportunities can lead to other things in life. My involvement at Southeast Missouri State University Department of Nursing and the remodeling of the old high school on campus led to either going from only a state-accredited program to being nationally accredited. We went to New York for this review and were accredited for the full three years. Quite an achievement! While there, the chair of the board of the National League of Nursing talked to me about starting a community health accreditation board for home health nursing and asked me if I would like to serve on this. I did for eight years.

Later, I was asked to serve on the Society for Women's Health Research in Washington, D.C., for six years. One initiative was to get women, and not only men, included in clinical trials.

A few years after this, I was notified I had been selected by Sen. Tommy Thompson, secretary of Health and Human Services, to serve on the National Institutes of Health, National Institute of Nursing Research Board. We were the final board to review research papers and decide what projects received government funding.

Over 22 years ago, the idea of the importance of women's health was at the forefront. Ann Knewitz, a registered dietitian, came to me because of other health conferences I was involved in. An administrator at Marion Memorial Hospital had been to a conference on this. We made a commitment to try a Southern Illinois women's health conference. Committees were formed, and we had a successful event. We had a lot of "selling" to do. But, remember, my husband and I are in the Pepsi business. We are used to selling.

I've been asked about my ongoing challenge with ovarian cancer. In 1996, when I was diagnosed, I was told I had maybe one to five years to live. I'm now on my 12th. My way of handling it was not asking, "Why me?" Instead, I knew I did not understand it, but I left it in the hands of God, who I knew had the answer. I have totally given the suffering and pain to him. He, in return, has given me such peace to deal with the overall disease. I keep on going on!

These last 12 years I've lived doing even more of the things I love. I'm a people person and love to share in their involvement in events. I continue to receive chemo treatments at present and daily I.V.s.

Once again, I refer to being open to opportunities. I was unaware, when I became involved in my community, that it would lead to the national boards involvement I became involved in because I enjoy public service to my community. The other was a by-product. This led to opportunities beyond my wildest dreams. In some way, I ask you to get involved if you are not at present.

I am deeply humbled and so appreciative of this honor bestowed on me tonight. You have certainly touched my heart and given me moments to remember.

Thank you.

Celebration of Life
for
Rosemary Berkel Crisp

February 22, 1937 – December 01, 2007

Eulogy

The following Eulogy was written by Cyndi and recited by Cyndi and Cheryl on behalf of all of Rosemary's family and friends:

Cyndi: Our Mother is Rosemary Berkel Crisp. She was born in Chicago, Illinois, the youngest of four children. She adored her parents and throughout her life remained close to her brother and two sisters. Her father was a welder, and her mother a homemaker. They were always involved in their church. One day some nuns came to their home and asked our mother if she'd consider joining a convent. "Do they have a band?" she asked. "No," they said. "Then, I can't," she replied, "because I really like being a baton twirler."

She had spunk. She had a spark about her.

Cheryl: Mom babysat for Dr. and Evvie Dibble during the summer, and she always said that watching Mrs. Dibble leave for work in her crisp, white nurse's uniform and cap sparked her interest in nursing. After getting her degree in college, she worked as night supervisor at Marion Memorial Hospital. During this time, she entered the Miss Marion Pageant; she says that they needed more contestants. At that event, she met our dad. Can you imagine a young man of 22 hanging around a beauty pageant?

She married our father on January 16, 1960, and in the years that followed, both the business and the family grew. Many times over the years we remember sitting around the dinner table. Mom and Dad would look at their six children and one would comment, "We really started something." The other would reply, "Yes, we really did." Six kids in 13 years. With all the ruckus at our house, it's amazing that Mom found time to teach us anything.

That is how her life started.

I guess if we had a theme to this eulogy, it would be little things make a difference. One person can make a difference.

Now, we'd really like to tell you about the woman that was our mother and your friend.

We were never with her in a restaurant or other public restroom when she didn't pick up toilet paper off the floor or dry around the sink to make it better for the next person. Think about that. It was a dirty job that could have been left for someone else. Also, the person she was doing it for never even saw her or knew she'd been there.

Why would she do that? She did it for God. It kept her humble, and it made the world a slightly better place for the next person.

Rosemary Crisp was innocent, yet knowledgeable; soft, yet strong; joyful, yet suffering. She did everything with God's will in mind. The number one thing Mom taught us was to put God first and give Him your best. She loved having her family around her. She loved her friends.

A gentleman came through during visitation yesterday. He said, "If you look in the dictionary under the word lady, it would say Rosemary Crisp." Dad and each of us want to thank you for the support you've shown to our family, in the stories you have shared with us about Mom, the cards you've sent, the love you've given.

Cyndi: The moments when you are with someone, be it once a year, once a month, once a week, once a day, or even all day, over time, create our relationships. We've always known that our mother loves people. It is in her nature and so much a part of her being that it extends to the paintings she enjoys, and the figurines she selected. "Look at that face," "See that expression?" she'd say. So I know how she felt about you, all of you. Whether you knew her from a meeting once a year or spent days with her every week, she really looked at your face. She really noticed your expression. If you cleaned her room or served her meals in the hospital, she probably would ask, "How is your day going?"

Cheryl: We would consider being a good wife and mother an accomplishment in itself. Being actively involved serving your community would be an accomplishment in itself. Mom did all these things and every one of them she did to the best of her ability. And, Mom was active. To name a few:

She was a Girl Scout Leader and volunteer nurse in our younger days. Her passion for nursing carried over later when she co-founded the Southern Illinois Women's Health Conference and also served on the board for the Hands of Hope Clinic. Education, another of my parents' endeavors, allowed her to serve on committees and boards of many colleges and universities in the area.

And Mom's level of involvement? She wouldn't just attend Women's Health Conference meetings, she was also involved

In the eulogy for Rosemary, Cyndi said Rosemary lived her life in the way that encouraged Harry L. to be the best he could be. His wedding band is inscribed with the words, 'Love is eternal.'

in selecting table arrangements and concerned about food taste. She wouldn't just attend Southeast Missouri State University, known as SEMO, nursing building meetings; she was also involved in restoring the original beauty of the building down to details such as the stain on the door frames. She always gave her best.

Cyndi: Mom truly believed she was just a young girl from Southern Illinois who was given opportunities. Whether sitting at a dinner at the White House or working on a university project, speaking at a church about her faith, or meeting the Pope, she kept her humble roots and faith in the Lord as her foundation.

One thing seemed to lead to another.

As I said earlier, she was involved in the SEMO nursing program and they needed to get accredited. To help with that, she flew to Washington, D.C., and while there, she met with others involved in the National League of Nursing. Next, she was invited to serve there.

Why was she given opportunities such as this? I believe it was because she always gave it her best. To the "Nth" degree, she did everything to the best of her ability, and people wanted her to become part of the team. Others recognized the sincerity and effort she displayed. Mom was always surprised that they felt she was qualified for these positions.

As a side note, in her last days, one of the nurses caring for her asked, "Are you Rosemary Berkel Crisp?" "Yes," she replied. "I was able to get my nursing degree because of you," the nurse said. "I went to SEMO."

We can't talk about Mom without telling you how much she loved our dad. No matter how many years Mom had been married to Dad, she still wanted to look pretty for him. She really, sincerely does. She believed that you stand by your husband ... together you are a team. And she lived her life in the way that encouraged him to be the best he could be and have fun in the ways that were good. Inscribed in his wedding band is "Love is eternal" and, Dad, it is.

Dad also knew about Mom's determination. In fact, this week we heard a story from Dr. Brigitte Barrette, Mom's doctor at Mayo Clinic. She told us she frequently would let a team of medical doctors spend time looking at Mom's charts and her X-rays. "We cannot help her," was often their conclusion. "Now," Dr. Barrette would say, "I want you to meet her." After talking to Mom, and hearing how she kept living her life, about her faith in God, and seeing her determination, they would come back and find something to try. "For those doctors," Dr. Barrette continued, "she changed medicine."

Pope John Paul II once said, "Life is not living in the fullest without faith in God."

Mom, you've always prayed the Rosary, went to church, even when you were out of town, and put your problems in God's hands. "Why worry when you can pray?"

Mom recently had taken a personality test – this is a true story – and the person giving the test said, I don't know this woman, but she is remarkable. Remarkable.

"Why?" he was asked. "Because," he said, "she has a high desire to achieve along with a high level of patience. Most high achievers are typically impatient. Yes, this woman is remarkable."

Mom, you are remarkable to us, too. In a world where people often say, "Why me?" You would say, "Why not me?"

While we were being raised in a world of the "Me Generation," you have shown the importance of knowing … that divinity is not within us … but in devotion to God.

"Love is patient, love is kind, love always believes the best …" You are simply a living example of faith, hope and love.

Matthew 25:21: His Lord said to him, Well done, good and faithful servant. Enter thou into the joy of the Lord.

– December 2007

'I go, but I do not go. I go, but I am not absent.
I go, but my heart remains with you.'

— Pope John Paul II,
farewell to the faithful, Mexico City, 2002

Epilogue

Sitting with his wife during her final hours, Harry L. asked Rosemary what he would do without his best friend and lifelong partner.

"Talk to me every day," she said, softly.

And that he does, noting, "I feel her presence all the time."

He talks to her during Mass each week as well, asking for a candle on the altar to flicker if she's listening.

"Every time I've asked during the last three years, that's exactly what has happened," Harry L. says.

And he's checked. There are no air vents.

'When I am gone,
I want you to look
at the sunset and think of me.'

Rosemary's favorite expressions

Let go … and let God.

Why worry when you can pray?

Do unto others as you would have them do unto you.

I'll give you a suggestion, and you do as you please.

Every cloud has a silver lining.

Count your blessings.

If you don't succeed, try, try again!

If you are having a bad day, have a pity party. Cry for about five minutes and then get on with your day.

God's not through with me yet!

Never let the sun go down on an argument.

I just offer it up to God.

I've got my "get-up-and-go pants" on.

"Plant a seed" in someone else's mind, and then give it time to grow on its own.

Husbands often have to be the boss and in control at work. When they come home, let the little boy in them come out.

Take care of yourself and dress nicely.

Eat a good breakfast, do not miss Mass. Pray and read your Bible. Be involved in your community.

This too shall pass.

Don't "should" on me.

Don't forget your lipstick.

Get your butt to bobbin'.

Sleep with the angels. Good night.

Acknowledgements

My thanks to Harry L. Crisp II for his confidence in my abilities to create a fitting tribute to his wife. Thanks also to the Crisp children and to Rosemary's brother, Jim Berkel, for the time they devoted to interviews, the wonderful memories they shared and for their continuing input during this project.

This opportunity never would have occurred without the recommendation of Samuel Goldman, Chancellor Emeritus of Southern Illinois University in Carbondale. Courtesy of my "day job" at the university, I had the pleasure of working frequently with Dr. Goldman during his two years as chancellor. Many thanks for your confidence as well, Sam.

Everyone interviewed for this book was generous with their time, their memories and their emotions. I hope I have adequately conveyed the depth of their feelings for Rosemary.

Sadly, several of those people passed away before the publication of this book, including Rosemary's lifelong friend, Marilyn Cavaness of Marion, Illinois. Rosemary greatly admired Marilyn, who lived with several debilitating conditions. Marilyn's spirit, her will and her mind were strong, her smile genuine and her laugh contagious. Like Rosemary, she, too, was an inspiration to all who knew her.

Longtime friend and trusted editor Larry Davis graciously volunteered his time to read the manuscript and offer valuable insights. The manuscript was much improved thanks to his keen eye and attention to detail.

Material gathered through interviews with Rosemary that were recorded by Bonnie Marx, a writer with the SIU Alumni Association, is included in this book.

The Southern Illinoisan was a partner in this project; thanks to Publisher Bob Williams and Editor Gary Metro, as well as other members of their staff who contributed time and effort. A special note of appreciation to Cara Recine and Rhonda Ethridge for manuscript editing and outstanding design work. The finished product reflects their professionalism.

Finally, special thanks to Kevin Davis of Pepsi MidAmerica in Marion. Although his name is not on the front of this book, Kevin was instrumental throughout the entire process. He served as an advocate, provided contact information for key individuals, made the initial phone calls to many people to open doors for me, and ensured I had everything I could possibly need to bring this project to fruition – including spending many hours sifting and sorting through photos and files. I am grateful for all of his insights and contributions, and for his friendship.

Tom Woolf
August 2011